The Widow,
The Priest
and
The Octopus
Hunter

For Paul, who also chose this island life.

Shiraishi Isle
Jellyfish on the water's edge
In the mist
—Nissho, 1969

translated by Roger Pulvers

AMY CHAVEZ

The Widow, The Priest and The Octopus Hunter

Discovering a Lost Way of Life on a Secluded Japanese Island

TUTTLE Publishing

Tokyo | Rutland, Vermont | Singapore

Published by Tuttle Publishing, an imprint of Periplus Editions (HK) Ltd.

www.tuttlepublishing.com

Copyright © 2022 Amy Chavez

Library of Congress Control Number: 2021949515

ISBN 978-4-8053-1691-7

26 25 24 23 22
10 9 8 7 6 5 4 3 2 1
2112TO

Printed in Malaysia

Distributed by:

North America, Latin America & Europe
Tuttle Publishing
364 Innovation Drive
North Clarendon
VT 05759 9436, USA
Tel: 1(802) 773 8930
Fax: 1(802) 773 6993
info@tuttlepublishing.com
www.tuttlepublishing.com

Asia Pacific
Berkeley Books Pte Ltd
3 Kallang Sector #04-01
Singapore 349278
Tel: (65) 6741-2178
Fax: (65) 6741-2179
inquiries@periplus.com.sg
www.tuttlepublishing.com

Japan
Tuttle Publishing
Yaekari Building, 3rd Floor
5-4-12 Osaki Shinagawa-ku
Tokyo 141 0032 Japan
Tel: 81 (3) 5437 0171
Fax: 81 (3) 5437 0755
sales@tuttle.co.jp
www.tuttle.co.jp

Contents

Foreword 7

Introduction: A Day on the Port 11

The War Widow 19

The Stone Bridge Lady 27

The Former Postmaster 36

The Fish Trapper's Father 43

A Reluctant Innkeeper 48

The Pufferfish Widow and Yakutoshi 54

The Outsider 61

Mother of Eleven 68

The Cargo Ship Captain 75

The Okami 81

The Ferry Captains Who Moonlight As Priests 84

The Runaway 90

Four Chinese Brides 101

The Dance Director 107

Keeper of the Graves 112

The Octopus Hunter 120

Second Generation U-Turns 123

The Buddhist Priest 135

The Doll Maker 140

A Quarryman 148

The Tombstone Maker's Wife 155

The Go-Between 161

A War Widow's Daughter.. 169

Weekenders.. 172

The Stonecutter.. 175

An Accidental Hermit 183

The Last Two Junior High School Students....................... 190

Newspaper Delivery Man.. 196

Stay-at-Home Dad 202

The Foreigner 207

Eiko.. 216

Epilogue 220

Photo, illustration, text and translation credits
Photo insert pages 1–2, page 5 bottom, page 6–8, page 10, page 11 left and bottom; page 13 bottom, Amy Chavez. Page 3 top, page 4 top, page 11 top, page 15, courtesy Shiraishi Island Archives. Page 3 bottom, page 5 top, courtesy Tetsumi Amano. Page 4, bottom courtesy Okae Harada. Page 12, courtesy Fumiyo Harada. Photo insert page 9, courtesy Masako Harada. Page 13 top, courtesy Tadashi Amano. Page 14 bottom, courtesy Mitsuko Amano. **Illustrations** page 28, 56, 165, 191, Okae Harada. Page 121, Lauralee Garson. **Text and translations** Page 194 Shiraishi Junior High School Song and pages 214, 215 *hauta* songs translated by Roger Pulvers. Page 117 and 130 Heart Sutra translations and permission to reprint by Alex Kerr.

Foreword

I MOVED TO JAPAN in 1993 after finishing an MA in Teaching English as a Second Language in the US. I chose Japan because through my university's sister-school relationship, I could move seamlessly into a ready-made teaching career at a Japanese university. Thus I ended up in Okayama, a city on the Seto Inland Sea in western Japan.

Although I've grown up with privilege, I've always preferred the sweaty fragrance of a fisherman to an aromatic man in an Armani suit. My animal-loving mother taught me to fancy the street-smart mutt over the purebred in a pet-shop window. And my father hailed the value of a self-propelled kayak over the ability to board a cruise liner. As a result of this privileged upbringing, I've always been more interested in living life than reaping its rewards.

When I first moved to Japan, I chose to live in a house with no bath or shower attached, so that I could frequent the public bathhouse and learn bathing customs direct from the locals. As a side benefit, I also learned Japanese via the steam-dampened accents of my neighbors as they verbally jostled for positions in the tub and slung a barrage of dialect at me that bounced off the bathhouse walls. Even now when I speak Japanese, you can detect that humid, steam-soaked echo in my voice.

At that time, local bathhouses were still plentiful in Japan's timeworn, pre-World War II neighborhoods crowded with wooden houses hewn before anyone gave a thought to including bathing facilities. For denizens of such houses that had escaped the bombings, the ritualized evening bath was as satisfying as a trip to the local market where old friends meet up, gossip and brag about their grandchildren.

The dwelling I rented, itself a survivor of the war, boasted a Yamazaki Bakery on the first floor (with a live-in proprietress) while I occupied the six-tatami-mat room upstairs (about 98 square feet or 9 square meters) with a sink and a one-burner camping stove. No young, modern-day Japanese would have chosen such a neighborhood, such a house, or such a room that required the daily ritual of paying for the privilege of bathing in the same tub as your neighbors. When my father—a man who had sent me to all the best schools and even allowed me to take my horse to boarding school—came to visit and found the newly minted university lecturer living in a six-mat room no bigger than a horse stall, he was absolutely beside himself: his daughter had truly arrived.

Four years later, I and the proprietress of the Yamazaki Bakery (who, after closing her shop in the evenings, often accompanied me to the public bath), had to move out so the owner of the house could bulldoze it. A mobile phone shop now gleams, without a shred of humility, in its place. After years of living in the city, wooed daily by Japan's cleanliness, efficiency, and convenience, I found myself yearning for something more soul-enriching. And since I suddenly had to find a new place to live, I thought I'd look for an environment that was slower, gentler, and more attuned to nature. Maybe I was searching for the simplicity of Zen, or the unrefined beauty of wabi-sabi, or perhaps I was just romancing the ruggedness of the Japanese countryside: the realm of wandering poets, ancient rituals, and moon gazing. But I knew that I wanted to live Japan from the ground up: feel the texture of its soil and taste the bitter *goya* fresh off the vine. I endeavored to do more than sample the exquisitely arranged Japanese food on my plate; I wanted to know where it came from and how it was made. I was keen to heave a wooden mallet onto rice to pound out *mochi* cakes, forage for mountain plants, gather seaweed, and dig on the beach for *asari* clams. I longed to wake up in the springtime to the song of the Japanese bush warbler singing *hoke-ko-kyo*, to hear the *sha-sha-sha* of gentle rain on clay-tiled roofs, to relish the screech of cicadas in the summer heat. In the cool of winter I dreamed of running to the sound of wind blowing through a bamboo forest: the very dwelling place of over eight million Shinto gods still revered as rulers of the earth.

So I started searching. Eventually, I found all that and more on Shiraishi Island in the Seto Inland Sea, populated by 430 residents (at the time of writing), most of them elderly, some well into their nineties. The life here is that which only exists elsewhere in the past. Communications are basic, a reliance on community ties is expected. The people here who regard the past precious are also the few wise enough to hold on to it: a people so comfortable in their skin that they do not need to be more, have more, nor want more. A people who refuse to reinvent themselves, and to which, therefore, the city holds no lure. It is among these extraordinary people that I find myself again in a position of privilege.

For me, moving to Shiraishi was a chance to get up close and personal with island traditions, superstitions and folklore. I gradually began to realize that island life is a niche lifestyle under the wider genre of Japanese countryside living. Here, each season gives way to preparations for a festival, ceremony, planting or harvest, just like anywhere else in the countryside, but what marks our uniqueness is the isolation. Community bonds of village life are strong and no caprices escape unnoticed on this scrap of land hemmed in by shallow seas. The briny borders have preserved the island like a jar of pickles; traditions here have survived decades longer than their mainland-village counterparts.

When I set out to record the stories of the people who live on Shiraishi, I knocked on doors, sat in people's houses and gardens, had chats with them on the ferry, shared beers on the beach, invited them to my house for tea, met them at the community center, stood with them at the temple, and accompanied them through the cemetery in order to listen to their stories. I even went on a fishing expedition with the Octopus Hunter. I perused scrapbooks and wedding photos of people both alive and deceased, and peeked into kimono drawers, old cedar chests, and sheds. I listened for over a hundred hours, recorded these conversations, and then transcribed them. Lastly, I went through the painstaking process of translating these memories into English, which required a team of one research student, one Japanese language teacher, and a Buddhist priest to help me interpret the accents, customs and antiquated vernacular of locals who have been living for almost a century in relative isolation. The result is this book about a small island in the Seto Inland Sea whose stories span four periods of Japanese history: Taisho, Showa, Heisei and Reiwa, or the years from 1912 to 2021.

The first thing you'll notice about the people on Shiraishi is that most know each other by sobriquets. The Stone Bridge Lady's moniker (*ishibashi no obachan* in Japanese) is a result of the tiny footbridge one must cross to get onto her property. Panken is a name made from combining the name Ken with the word *pan* (bread) to denote the son of the family who owned the local bread shop. Other people are addressed by their occupations: Mr. Postmaster, Mr. Stonecutter or Mr. Buddhist Priest, or even by their positions: Dance Director, Local Councillor or Local Councillor's Wife. The suffix *chan*, usually reserved for children or good friends, is used liberally here—Kazu-chan, Mi-chan, Kio-chan—and expresses the close ties of the community. Those who own businesses are usually referred to by the name of their business: Amasaka, Amagiso and Otafuku, to give a few examples, can be either the business itself, or the person(s) running it. Once Panken, Mr. Postman, or Kio-chan, always so, even beyond retirement, until the day they die. Since this is how islanders refer to each other in everyday life, I have chosen to continue this tradition of familiarity in the book.

For now, the living past of Shiraishi Island carries on via these elders who can orally pass down their stories. But when these children of the early twentieth century pass away, they will not be replaced by sons, daughters or grandchildren because they have all moved to the cities. Only the boulders and mountains on this island will be witness to what once was.

Introduction
A Day on the Port

MY SECOND-FLOOR bedroom window looks out over twenty or so fishing vessels, five of them trawlers that put out to sea around five o'clock in the evening. With their high wooden prows and navy blue "eyes" hand-painted on their bows, the boats slip out past the port entrance one by one into the glow of the evening.

From midship, metal pipes angle skyward, peaking above the stern, a height from which, once at sea, the gathered orange nets cascade down to the water's surface like giant rooster tails. Anyone standing on Shiraishi Beach watching these trawlers glide across the horizon against a background of the tangerine setting sun will feel a pang of nostalgia for the pastoral fishing life that still exists on these small islets in the Seto Inland Sea.

The remaining boats in port are flat-bottomed and fiberglass. They are lined up, noses tethered to the dock, their stern anchors set. Their hulls clash and chafe in the wake of the incoming and out-going port traffic. The fishermen use these skiffs to dart back and forth between fish traps and to haul up nets from the deep. Low-lying gunwales allow nets and octopus pots to be easily pulled aboard, their contents unceremoniously dumped into the fish holds of the boat. Whereas the trawlers leave at sunset, the skiffs prowl out just as the black hues of night bleach into the ephemeral pastels of dawn. Slowly and stealthily the fishermen come and go, just like the tides. My life is synched to the twenty-four-hour activities of these fisherfolk.

On summer nights, when I'm snuggled in bed with windows wide open to the port, I drift off to sleep in the soft shore breeze that dances lightly across me as though wafting a clean white sheet on a laundry line.

If it's after midnight on a Friday, my slumber is accompanied by the sound of the Kaisei Maru cargo ship releasing its anchor in the offing: the heavy chunk of metal races down towards the bottom of the sea, and the thick links of chain whir around the winch—clankety clank, clankety clank—until a thick and abrupt silence envelopes the air, indicating the anchor has hit bottom. With the ship's propeller still softly bub-bub-bubbing in the water, the captain engages the gears, and the boat glides back, back, back until the anchor chain is taut and the hulking vessel is arrested. The anchor now set, the Cargo Ship Captain cuts the engine, bringing another soft and absolute silence. He flicks off the navigation lights, switches on the single white anchor light at the top of the mast, then he and his brother climb into their dinghy and lower themselves by mechanical winch to the water alongside the 200-foot (58-meter) long ship. Once the waves swell up under their little craft, they unclip it from the shrouds, and the dinghy slips soundlessly through the darkness into the safety of the port.

In the adolescent hours of dawn, the soft gurgle of a churning propeller wakes me from the depths of sleep. I rise to the surface of consciousness, as if a diver slowly making her way up through water. I take in a deep breath of air, and sit up. My curtains stand open as I have left them and I watch the scene outside my window come into focus as if being slowly exposed in a darkroom.

The turn of the propeller that has coaxed me out of sleep belongs to a boat tethered to the dock below my window. The Fish Trapper is readying his idling boat, and has released the docking lines. Wearing a yellow T-shirt and tan trousers with hems stuffed into the top of white rubber boots, he nudges the gear shift into reverse and the small flat-bottomed boat glides languidly out of the slip with a big yawn. The Fish Trapper, agile the way only fishermen are, steps into his waterproof fishing gaiters leg by leg, and pulls them up over his trousers while the boat whispers in reverse over small ripples of agitated water. Overalls now fastened, he shifts the engine into forward. The Fish Trapper leans against the captain's chair and crosses his arms over his chest as the boat ambles past the red flashing light of the harbor entrance and out to sea.

The port itself is small, a quarter of a mile (391 meters) long, and the width less than half that. A professional Japanese archer could sling an arrow from one side of the port and hit one of the houses on the other. When standing at the ferry terminal and looking towards my house one cannot fail to notice that at the top of the mountain in back of my house is a boulder that sticks up awkwardly like a gem that has wriggled free from its gold setting. This upright stone is named Bikuni, and is the first piece of granite on this stone-speckled island to feel the caress of the sun at dawn and the last to reflect her golden beams in evening. This designation deems Bikuni a sacred rock according to Japan's indigenous Shinto religion. Every port entry and exit is performed under the venerable gaze of Bikuni.

While the Japanese haiku poet Matsuo Basho was writing his famous travel diary *Narrow Road to the Interior*, local laborers on Shiraishi Island were mining the island granite by hammering iron pegs into stones until they split. These smaller pieces of stone were hand-chipped into blocks, and fitted on top of each other to reinforce the harbor walls and to make two jetties on opposite sides of the port. These two lobster claws leave enough of a gap for one ferry to pass or two small fishing boats to squeeze through, one entering while the other exits. Behind each jetty a mountain rises, forming a forested gateway into the harbor.

After the Fish Trapper's boat has disappeared, a small motorbike with a clunky old fish tray strapped on the back putters down the strip of bitumen between my house and the dock. Mr. Kawata maneuvers his Honda Super Cub down a wooden plank and onto the pontoon with guided precision, and comes to a stop. In one fluid movement he hops off, thrusts down the kickstand with the heel of his rubber boot and drops down into a boat so small, it sits lower than the top of the dock. Already inside the boat waiting is his nephew Ma-kun, who has been smoking a cigarette while watching the dawn appear. The old man releases the pre-knotted loops of rope fore and aft, then with a simple turn of the key, the engine sputters to life and he and Ma-kun are putt-putting out past the lighthouse, fast in the Fish Trapper's wake.

Now it's six fifteen and the sun, having already ascended the mountain in back of my house, is casting its golden hue onto Tomiyama Hill on the other side of the port. The sun's warmth kisses awake nesting herons in the treetops and tints their alabaster wings gold.

While evenings are marked by the riplets of the tide, the mornings are still, as if time's relentless pull forward has been stayed. The tide now high, between my house and the opposite side of the port is only water, placid as morning dew. This shadow pond mirrors everything above it: the amber sky, a passing gossamer cloud, a seagull circling figure eights. In these early hours life is reflected, duplicated and copied a thousand times a minute, in burst mode, recording a life of softer lines and breathtaking quietude. It is a temporary lull, and my favorite time of day.

By now I am standing downstairs in the living room with the windows open. I watch as the curtain of light creeps down the side of the mountain, having dropped below the treetop herons. As the sun inches its way down through the shroud of darkness, the outline of Bikuni Rock looms ominously, casting a craggy, creeping ghost shadow of itself onto the mountain opposite. *Shiraishi* means "white stone" and refers to the rocks like Bikuni that dot the mountainscape. It goes without saying that if there are so many boulders on top of the mountain, there are just as many along the shoreline. These wave-worn behemoths encircle thousands of islands in the Seto Inland Sea, their imposing presence a defense against the vagaries of winds and waves. My small house on the breakwater was constructed on top of such boulders, some of which had no doubt fallen from above sometime in the past. Their inevitable plummet is predicated by centuries of typhoons and landslides that have, and always will, encourage the mountain to shed its accessories. Occasionally still, a boulder plows through someone's living room.

A cormorant standing on the gunwales of a fishing boat wiggles its behind and opens its wings to dry them in the anticipated warmth of the sun. Wings stretched, he rocks from foot to foot, moving to his own rhythm, twitching his tail feathers as if Japan's mythical sun goddess herself has just pushed open the door of her heavenly rock cave to bring light into the world. Now, the magic is about to happen.

When the sun's warmth hits the cooled night air cradled between the mountain walls of the port, this cool air mass begins to move. The newly warmed air expands, pushing the cool air into a single-pulse breeze that rushes across the water's surface to my side of the port where it blasts through my living room window. The effect lasts mere moments, but this swelling, surging billowing of cool air is one of the natural miracles that happens every day on this small island.

With the official dawning of the day, a *bora* fish jumps from the water's surface at the angle of sleet in a strong wind, and slaps its body down—kersplash!—to rid its scaly body of sea lice. The leggy gray herons take up their sentinel positions on the gunwales of docked fishing boats, standing motionless on their bobbing perches while awaiting the return of the Fish Trapper, Mr. Kawata and Ma-kun with their catches and occasional breakfast handouts. The cormorants are back in the water, disappearing into the depths, only to surface a half minute later before diving again.

The sun, now high in the sky, reflects off the water like a million fluttering eyes opening their lids first thing in the morning. Ripples of tension in the water's surface signal that the tide has started to move; the port empties out gradually, in the manner of a bottle of fine wine. The outgoing tide, though invisible to the untrained eye, will lower the boats 13 feet (4 meters) over the next six hours.

The first commercial boats arrive from the mainland just before seven o'clock, stopping only long enough for the hobby-fishermen to pick up bait from the pontoon in front of the Fishermen's Union for a day of single-pole angling. Each boatload carries four to eight customers bundled in yellow life jackets. They lounge on the gunwales while the captain sidles his boat up to the pontoon and a tall middle-aged fisherman with a crop of slightly curly graying hair takes a bucket and scoops out some small bait fish from his trawler's holding tanks. He hands the full pail to his exuberant wife who smiles and passes it back to the waiting captain. As he steers the boat away from the dock, the next boat full of customers sidles in.

At about this time, a young skinny guy in scuffed white rubber boots and turquoise waterproof overalls arrives on the dock with a cigarette hanging from his mouth, looking like the fishermen's version of the Marlboro Man. He is the Octopus Hunter, heading out in his skiff to check his traps. When he returns in an hour, he'll transfer over a dozen fresh captives into orange netted bags that allow the crafty mollusks to stay alive in the holding nets cast over the side of the boat. Later he will sell them to inns on the island who serve fresh seafood to mainlanders staying overnight on a weekend getaway.

If it's a Thursday, the islanders will start trundling past my window with empty fuel containers loaded into hand carts. This is the only day of the week the local populace can buy fuel for their vehicles or kerosene for their heaters in winter. They'll line up their marked cans outside the pumps at the Fishermen's Union, and go home for breakfast. When an employee arrives from the mainland on the 7:45 ferry, she'll fill the cans with fuel and collect payment when the containers are fetched by their owners, all before she leaves on the noon ferry to disappear for another week.

The Fish Trapper and Mr. Kawata return after checking their individual fish traps. The Fish Trapper keeps his fish in his boat's holds while Mr. Kawata stands near the dock icing down some recently expired corpses. Ma-kun is already walking home past my house, carrying a large plastic bag holding two large fish, noses facing the ground and black tails flapping out the top. Mr. Kawata heads home too, his fish laid out on the fish rack on the back of his motorbike.

The day starts for non-fishers when the ferry ticket personnel arrive. The small booth is manned by either Yakutoshi, who recently moved back to the island to care for his ninety-five-year-old mother, or Takanori, who retired five years ago from a job on the mainland and chose to move back (with his wife) to their home island. These two returnees take turns working the ticket counter.

The first passenger ferry headed to the mainland enters the port at 7:05 a.m. The service starts at Manabe (population 120), the outermost island in the Kasaoka island chain, where the captain lives. It will make momentary landings at Kitagi Island (population 700), Shiraishi Island (population 430), Takashima Island (population 100), and Konoshima Island (population 10,000) before finally reaching the city of Kasaoka on the mainland. From there it will immediately embark on the reverse course, alighting for a few moments on each island in the chain.

Next to toot its horn upon arrival is the school boat. Four elementary schoolchildren climb on board, and head off to school on the nearby island of Konoshima. Dropping off their charges are two grandfathers and one father, Makoto Amano, who, while seeing off two schoolchildren carries a newborn in a harness slung across his chest. They stand on the pontoon until the school boat is out of sight.

At exactly 7:47 the first ferry from the mainland enters the port. Bound newspapers and a mail bag are chucked off the boat while six school staff members disembark. They include four teachers who teach the two island children who attend the junior high school.

All arriving passengers to Shiraishi Island are greeted by a stone monument announcing that this is the home of the "Shiraishi Bon Dance—Intangible Folk Cultural Property." The large slab of rock mounted with its flat polished side facing the newcomers is inlaid with a black-and-white photo of locals in costume dancing their traditional dance to appease the souls of the warriors who perished in the Inland Sea naval battle in 1185 as told in the epic *Tale of the Heike*.

The last option for a morning commute to the mainland is the car ferry—captained by a father-son duo—that leaves the port at 8:00 a.m. It carries mostly passengers going shopping for the day or those who are leaving the island after having spent a few days here. Most islanders don't have cars and the few who do tend to keep them on the mainland to avoid the ferry fees required to bring them back and forth. Luggage and larger purchases are easier to load and unload via the loading ramp onto the car ferry. Residents such as the Buddhist Priest can board while still on his scooter when going to conduct funerals on the mainland, and Taiko-san (the Mother of Eleven) atop her four-wheeled electric cart can drive right off at the other end to get to her medical appointments. Mimiko, one of our summer residents, prefers this ferry when returning to Tokyo because the ferry personnel will send her suitcases on to the capital straight from the boat, freeing her up to carry her two cats, each in its own pet carrier, to the train station for the four-hour bullet-train ride back to the city.

Soon after the ferry departs, I hear a swish and a slap as the Newspaper Delivery Man slides open my door and drops the paper on the entryway step. As I peruse the morning news, a bewhiskered man heads out to sea with his beagle named Hime ("Princess") standing at the stern of his private fishing boat, snuffling the air. Once in the middle of the port he thrusts his craft into neutral. As the boat patiently waits, he walks to the stern, faces west, claps his hands twice and bows to the Buddhist deity *namikiri-fudo* (wave-calming Fudo-myo-o), an ancient image etched over eight hundred years ago into the rock along the west side of the port, an early example of the island's rock worship. After praying for safe seas, a tradition performed since times of yore, he and Hime slip out of the port. This man always returns safely, but not all fishermen do. He is one of the lucky ones.

At nine forty-five on Tuesdays and Thursdays, a doctor from the mainland alights to offer his services at the island clinic from ten in the morning to four in the afternoon.

By eleven the activity on the port has quieted to just a few wheeled carts, a bicycle or two and the occasional pedestrian. Docked boats are commandeered by seagulls enjoying the mid-morning lull. At lunchtime, an unusual silence takes over as life no longer moves, but just floats. No ferries come in or go out, no boats strain on their ropes, and even the occasional small fishing boat sneaks into the port like duck paddling through a silent wake. The stillness seems to linger even as the first afternoon ferry comes in. On the high tide, a music-box chime drifts out of the interior of the ferry as it crosses the water, announcing to passengers that this stop is Shiraishi Island.

All this happens outside my window every day. The humming of the ferries trundling back and forth with their passengers predictably getting on and off, fades in and out like background music. At any point I can look out the window and recognize the movements as if they were hands on a clock. The toots of the ferries, the back draft as the ferry propeller reverses, the tinkling of the arrival chime drifting across the port, all combine to make a day on the island complete.

The War Widow

"YOU'RE SURE YOU WON'T BE lonely living here all by yourself?" chuckles the skinny-armed man whose white forearms jut out of his plaid, short-sleeved button-down shirt as he stabs a long aluminum key into the back door. His slim waist is encircled by a belt that sits so low on his hips his pants hang a little too far down over his dress shoes. "I can't imagine why an American would want to live out here on an island like this in the middle of nowhere. You gotta admit, it's a bit unusual."

I assure him I'll be fine although, in truth, I'm a bit anxious. I have agreed to rent this house without having seen the inside of it. All I know is that the small, two-story home on the breakwater will be rented to me as is.

It's 1997, and the house has been vacant for six months after the man's mother, showing signs of needing elder care, went to live with her son on the mainland. Today, the three generations—the seventy-seven-year-old matron, her only son, his wife, and the sole grandchild—have come back to perform a ritual house cleaning before handing over the keys.

There have been no formal introductions, and we awkwardly bow and smile to each other while the wife with a short pixie hair-cut distributes gloves and cleaning supplies to me and her thirteen-year-old daughter. The grandmother stands patiently, eyes focused on the door.

"You know that when typhoons come, you can be stuck here for days," continues the son, still fiddling with the key. We're all standing too close for comfort on the walkway outside the back of the house, squeezed between a slab of igneous rock that buffers the mountain behind and delineates the national park that butts up to the back of the house. At the end of the walkway is a young Chinese fan palm lending just enough of a subtropical touch to tinge the atmosphere with an island glow. "The last ferry from the mainland is at six o'clock. You won't be able to stay in town and party with your friends in the evenings."

"Mmm."

The lock finally clicks, he slides open the door and we file into the sleeping house, moving through ghostly breaths of stale air. After removing my shoes in the light filtering through the sliding door, I follow cautiously behind the others who stumble through the dark kitchen and onto tatami mats. Finally, the son tugs at a string hanging down in the middle of the room and a round halogen lamp light sputters to life, exposing the contents of the room in brief flashes as if stuck between past and present.

When the light hums a consistent white, I take in my surroundings. Frosted-glass window panes block out the view of the port while the transparent glass of china cabinets exposes jumbled glassware and towers of bowls stacked at awkward angles. Traditional *shoji* doors dividing the rooms are not filled with the usual white paper, but with opaque glass chiseled with snowflake patterns. The panes clatter in their frame whenever the doors are slid open or closed. The few walls that don't double as windows or sliding doors are painted a frozen-pea green—with sparkles. The only two chairs in the room are upholstered in plastic in hues of unripened lime. The stainless-steel kitchen sink, olive-colored refrigerator and the aging gas burners on the stove are surrounded by faded pink walls, and more frosted windows. The kitchen floor is linoleum and orange.

From her tote bag, the wife produces a large pack of city-issued garbage bags which she snaps open with rubber-gloved fingers as she starts chucking fifty years of trinkets, bobbles, souvenir pens, dusty one-yen coins, and stray hairpins. She is ruthless, probably having wanted to do this for a long time. Items are shoveled up with cupped hands and tossed into the bags, which are carefully tied, as if taking restaurant left-overs home to a Saint Bernard.

Meanwhile the grandmother sits perfectly poised in the ladylike *seiza* position, legs tucked beneath her, on the tatami-mat floor in front of a low tea table under the halogen lamp, disinterested in the activity swirling around her. When an aluminum kettle whistles from the kitchen, she gets up to make green tea.

"The only good thing about this house is the view of the sea," says my new landlord, while a sickly pale glow emanates from the frosted window panes facing the port.

"Eiko-chan!" hollers an elderly woman from the front door. "Eiko-chan, welcome back!" A boisterous woman advances straight through the house, obviously familiar with its layout. She steps into the kitchen and the two old ladies chatter, the former eager to find out about Eiko's new life on the mainland, a place not many of the elderly islanders have ever lived. Tea is served at the low table while the two former neighbors continue to catch up on the latest news. Someone cracks open one of the windows facing the port to let in fresh air and I can see a sliver of life outside in the sea that is the front yard: a boat sliding by, leaving behind a wake of froth in a V-shape as if at the head of a flock of birds. It soon disappears behind frosted glass. Up near the cornice of the ceiling, a portrait leans down from above: Hirohito, the Showa emperor, and his wife, Nagako.

"The toilet is down the hall," the landlord calls over to me, neglecting to show me the details of what I already know is a non-flush, pit-style toilet like all the others on the island. You squat over this hole, then replace the cover over the cesspit when you're finished. Sanitary workers come to clean out the fetid waste once a month with trucks ringed in spiraled vacuum tubes.

"C'mon, I'll show you upstairs." We pad up the amply spaced wooden stairs made of keyaki wood, with their smooth, polished feel under my stockinged feet. We leave footprints in the fine coating of dust.

At the top of the stairs is a circular framed brush painting of Mount Fuji, the mountain which, Edwin Bernbaum wrote, "symbolizes the quest for beauty and perfection that has shaped so much of Japanese culture, both secular and sacred." Opening the sliding doors to the right of the sacred mountain sends their glass panes quivering in their frames, and I find myself in a room surrounded by large, clear-paned windows on three sides. At the back of the house, the forest is so close I can almost touch the branches of its trees reaching over the wall of rock towards the window. It's like being in the top of a lighthouse. Beyond the port, the Inland Sea stretches out several miles before my eyes until it meets the misty chocolate hills of the next island in the chain. Cargo ships drift past, their small lights pulsing from their masts, herons perch on fishing buoys and cormorants bob in the water's wake. I no longer care about the linoleum floor, the pit toilet or the plastic upholstered chairs.

At the end of the day, with the surface cleaning accomplished, there is still much of the old lady's stuff in closets. But since I am just renting the house, there is no pressing need to clean out everything in one day.

"Use whatever you like and what you don't want, you can throw out," the landlord tells me. Though the shelves were stuffed with everything from old futons and linens to housewares, it seemed that anything valuable had been removed. The furniture and stacks of dishes were what would be needed by almost anyone moving to an island, since there are no stores here to purchase such things.

After that, and not without some initial trepidation, they handed over their home to this foreigner, who still had much to learn about island ways.

For me, moving into this house was a chance to get up close and personal with island traditions, superstitions and folklore. I gradually began to realize that island life is a niche lifestyle under the wider genre of Japanese countryside living. On this island, no bridges breathe new life in or out, no mountain streams bring fresh water, and there is no proverbial sound of frogs singing from rice paddies. Fishermen's wives replace farmers' wives, and countryside farmhouses are, instead, seaside cottages with their windows facing in, rather than out over the expansive sea that brings tempests and typhoons.

What I didn't know at the time was that Eiko, the grandmother, born in the ninth year of the Taisho period (1920), had married one year before the end of World War II. Her husband had been immediately drafted into the Imperial Japanese Army and the newly married couple were separated. He would soon die in battle, never to meet the child his wife was carrying.

When the baby was born, Eiko was already a widow. Her son—my landlord—grew up with no father, no siblings, and almost no extended family, while most of his peers came from large families of eight to ten children. Eiko worked at a local inn to make ends meet. After junior high school on the island, her son had little choice but to forgo high school to find a job. At fifteen, he took an apprenticeship with a ferry company, and, like the father he never knew, worked on boats. He later became captain of a small passenger ferry plying the waters of the Inland Sea.

All this I learned the next week upon moving into the house and meeting some of my neighbors. And so it was that I took over a home not just brimming with the old lady's possessions, but also the son's memories of an unsettled childhood and the grandchild's sparse reminiscences of weekend visits to grandma's house, each visit marked by a bout of seasickness. As if such ambivalence was not enough, in an act deemed scandalous by almost every other islander, the widow left behind her deceased husband's *ihai*, or spirit tablet, on the household family altar.

❈ ❈ ❈

In 2003, I attended the funeral for Eiko. She had gone on to live six more years after having left her house on Shiraishi. The funeral invitation was a token gesture by the son and his wife, and naturally I felt honored to be asked to attend.

The ceremony was held by the island's Buddhist Priest at a funeral hall on the mainland, after which we accompanied the body to the crematorium. Hours later, the son carried the urn, and in a small hexagonal white and gold brocade box, his mother's Adam's apple. (In Japan, the larynx is revered as a small Buddha.)

On the forty-ninth day after death, when Buddhists believe reincarnation takes place, Eiko's son, his wife and their child brought the urn back to Shiraishi Island to be interred. I remember standing around the final resting place with the family, that small clan of three, while the Buddhist Priest lit candles, burned incense and chanted sutras while placing the urn inside the ossuary of the small tomb.

At that time, the son finally removed the father's spirit tablet from the Buddhist altar in the house and carried it back to his home. He did not, however, take away anything else from the house.

It was also around this time that he agreed to sell me the home I had been renting for six years. The time had come to move Eiko's remaining boxes from the closets upstairs into the shed outside.

❀ ❀ ❀

Someone else in my position would surely have gone through the entire house as soon as it was handed over to them, ridding themselves of the other person's tastes, artistic preferences, and outmoded cooking utensils. But not me. I had kept it all.

I became accustomed to living amongst the belongings of this woman I never knew, a war widow I had met once and whose funeral I had attended. A woman whose presence was still keenly felt in the lacquered zelkova table I placed my tea cup on, in the wall-hanging of Mount Fuji at the end of the hallway, the hanging scroll in the *tokonoma* alcove and the picture of the Showa emperor, Hirohito, looking ominously down from the cornice of the ceiling. I washed my hands in the water running from Eiko's faucets, cooked in her kitchen and slept with the sea breeze blowing through her bedroom window. I came in and out of the same door that shut each year end, and opened every New Year.

Over the years, as my husband and I renovated the house one room at a time, certain crannies would need to be cleared out, such as the small cupboard under the stairway, or the enclosed area in back of sliding doors under the Buddhist altar where the accouterments for prayers and vigils are kept: prayer bowls, candles, incense, photos of the deceased.

Such hideaways were crammed with boxes filled with items carefully wrapped in kanji-lettered newspaper from 1957, 1962, 1970.

Each parcel required holding, weighing, while caressing its smooth curves and sharp corners, before unwrapping, observing, postulating, and deciding to pitch or not. But I was hardly the person to be wielding such decisions. Who was I to decide the fate of someone else's possessions, to judge their intrinsic value based on years of joy and sorrow?

It was this hesitancy to take on the authority of deciding the fate of someone else's possessions, as well as a moral barrier I had to leap each time I delved into the private matters of someone else, that kept me from further uncovering the remnants of the widow's life. It wasn't until 2020, when my husband and I embarked on a final round of renovations to the house that we decided time had come to go through Eiko's remaining boxes and perhaps give her son a chance to claim anything he wanted before disposing of them.

By now I had come to view the past with a more sympathetic lens. I relished the glimpses of a time long gone and considered these memorabilia gold nuggets yearning to be discovered, indulged in and used to celebrate the life of a war widow in rural Japan. With each new realization, I was newly fascinated, and tried to imagine what life had been like for Eiko.

I peered into boxes full of identical ceramic rice bowls and green-tea cups, most likely used to entertain neighbors and guests at weddings, funerals and other major life events. Some of the ceramic patterns suggested celebration, such as maple leaves tinted gold, while others were more introspective, such as boys in Chinese dress chasing butterflies. There was a set of four black lacquer stackable boxes used for special New Year food, with a motif of gold-leaf cranes. In addition, there was a rather large cardboard carton overflowing with sparkly branches that looked like Christmas decorations, but weren't. I unpacked decorative Chinese zodiac animals (each to be displayed in the *tokonoma* alcove during its particular calendar year). I discovered an indigo *yukata* summer kimono with white *sashiko* hand-stitching; a bright yellow cotton kimono of an abstract design indicative of garments of the 1950s; a pair of wooden *geta* sandals for both a man and a woman. There was memorabilia: pine-wood rice scoops with red-dipped handles branded with the sacred name of Mount Koya; a square wooden sake cup engraved on one panel; and a paper fan advertising the business "Amano Masagoro Shoten, telephone number: 15." I spotted a soft blue *kaya* mosquito net, sections of it black with grit, and a paper bag stuffed with half a dozen pairs of shoes for a tiny woman's feet, size three. I found boat journals, English study books, a manila envelope brimming with sundry receipts. And I uncovered a schoolboy's tin box of calligraphy tools, including an inkstone, and brushes soaked stiff with sixty-year-old black ink. At the bottom of one box, I found a very small girl's kimono and a decorative cart and ox of the type usually displayed with Hina Matsuri dolls for the annual Girls' Day celebration. It was as if someone had shoved their heart into the darkest corners of the house for safe keeping. Or was it to forget?

I found myself wanting to know more about this woman who left her soldier husband's spirit tablet behind on the Buddhist altar of the house to reside with an American girl who was not only a stranger, but a sure progenitor of the enemy who had killed him.

Thus sparked with new curiosity, I embarked on the task of interviewing as many of the island's mostly elderly residents as I could to compile this oral history of Shiraishi Island and a war widow named Eiko, that you are about to read.

The Stone Bridge Lady

THE BUSH WARBLERS are announcing spring as I cross a small stone bridge into an old Japanese garden for my first interview. A stone lantern peeks out from behind a pine tree with a wrinkled bark. The branch of a *babe* tree is being pulled hither by an anchored rope to encourage growth in this direction. I press the doorbell and moments later hear a door slide open at the far side of the garden. A woman with golden white hair, grasping a prettily painted cane peers out. She tells me to wait while she comes around to the front door.

Once I'm invited inside, the Stone Bridge Lady opens the *shoji* paper-screened doors onto a cavernous twelve-tatami-mat room off the entrance. "I used to entertain people in this room but with my bad knee now, I can't sit on the floor anymore." I peer into the elegant space: a large calligraphic scroll hangs in the alcove; fresh, white shoji doors suggest another room beyond, and oh, what's that hulking in the corner? A life-size statue with a menacing face, wearing armor: it's a samurai! A horned helmet sits atop the head, a sword hangs to his side, ready to butt and lance the first intruder. Leaning down from above is a framed photo of a dapper-looking man who must be her deceased husband. "The house is seventy years old," she explains. "We built it after we married." Her voice echoes down the polished wooden-floored corridor as she leads me to the back of the fourteen-room house and ushers me into a room with a Western-style sofa.

"I was born in Taisho 14 [1925], you know. I'm ninety-five. Not many of my classmates are still around. I'm one of four children, all girls. I'm the youngest and the only one left.

"In the Meiji period [1868–1912], my father was a fisherman. But then all the men had to go to war so they couldn't continue fishing. My father had to go too. Those of us born in the Taisho era [1912–1926], we had a tough time. There were always wars going on. When

27

I was in elementary school, we had the Chinese Incident—our war with China—then when I was in high school there was the Pacific War. Our top military man at that time was Tojo Hideki.

"It was just after the war, during the US Occupation, when I married Ryosaku. His father and mine were cousins. At that time, when women married, they always went to the bridegroom's house and lived there. The oldest son would live in the same house as his parents and the younger brothers would set up a new household somewhere else—this system is called *honke-bunke*. The word *honke* refers to the parents' house, the family heritage home. Since I married the first son, I moved here into the honke house. I also took care of his parents as they aged.

"But eventually we tore down the old place and built this one, so the garden is much older than the house. I grew up in a different neighborhood, in Okujo. My family home is vacant now because my sisters went to live with their husbands when they married. I pay someone to cut the weeds around that house, but no one lives there.

"My husband went to Iwakuni with the Marine Corps for some years. It wasn't until he came back that I married him. I was twenty-three years old and he was one year older than me. At that time, no one owned much of anything. My mother bought me a kimono

to get married in. I don't know how she found it or how she paid for it but I remember it was black with a pattern of Japanese maple leaves. The sleeve length was somewhere in between the long ones that an unmarried woman wears and the shorter sleeves of a married woman. This kimono with mid-length sleeves is called *chuburi*. After that, my younger relatives all borrowed mine. Seems like everyone got married in that kimono! But people don't wear chuburi anymore. I have it somewhere in a drawer.

"We spent two or three days getting ready for the wedding. In those days all functions were carried out at home, so my wedding was here. In those days getting married to someone who lived on the island was normal. We often married our cousins, so we all have the same name: Harada, Amano, Nishihara, Nakatsuka, Yamakawa. Lots of them!

"Anyway, after we married, I couldn't get pregnant. My husband really, really wanted a child so he talked to his brother about adopting one of his sons. But by then the brother had moved to the mainland and his wife didn't care for Shiraishi Island, so in the end, she wouldn't let the child come here and live with us. Well, we're an island so the life is different here.

"So then we thought we could adopt one of my older sister's sons, but that didn't work out either. You know that samurai statue in the front room? That's the traditional ornament to display in the house on the annual Boy's Day celebration in May. We bought that because we thought we would be adopting my nephew."

※ ※ ※

At the turn of the seventeenth century there were an estimated fifty houses on Shiraishi Island. In the Meiji period (1868–1912) when Japan first started to modernize and divided itself according to prefectures, this island, previously of the Fukuyama-Bingo feudal domain, was assigned to Okayama Prefecture. At that time, more houses were built along the port and the harbor was soon full of fishing vessels. On the west side, fishers tied up their wooden boats in front of their houses and used the stone steps engineered into the walls to climb up to their homes. The Fishermen's Union sits on the east side of the port.

Nothing much changed geographically on Shiraishi from then until the years immediately following World War II and the US Occupation, when the island modernized by laying down a road for vehicles around the perimeter of the port that allowed people to travel over a paved surface. In addition, more remote areas of the island previously only accessible by mountain footpaths were soon linked by a 4-mile (6 km) ring road that follows the coastline.

The Stone Bridge Lady has seen a lot of changes on the island in her ninety-five years. "When I was a child, there was just a skinny dirt road along the port. The water came right up to your shoes. I was in high school when they changed all that. Those houses on the west side of the port weren't there either. It was all sea. The east side too! Your house wasn't there. Now there's that nice road that goes in front of your place to the Fishermen's Union. Before there was only the pilgrimage path that went out to the point.

"Ryosaku was on the local council, you know. He worked so hard. He had a tough job. You know the road that goes around the island along the beach past the inns? He made that road in 1967. Well, he didn't do it himself, but he was responsible for putting the plan into action. So now people can drive to the beach from the port rather than having to walk through the middle of the island to get there.

"My husband did a lot of good things for the island. It was a prosperous time after the war, so whatever he thought the island needed, he was able to procure. Water, for example. Before, there were only wells on the island. We had two wells on our property so we were fine, but others didn't have a well. The seaweed fishermen needed fresh water for cleaning the seaweed and the rock quarries needed it for cutting the rock. If you just cut rock while dry, sparks fly so it's dangerous. They couldn't use salt water either, it had to be fresh.

"It was a real problem in the summertime during the Bon festival of the dead when everyone needs water for the ritual washing of the gravestones. We had to carry buckets of water on poles over our shoulders all the way up that Tomiyama Hill to the cemetery. People who had lots of graves to look after had a hard time. People were constantly arguing over water.

"When we got running water piped in from the mainland, finally there was enough water and people stopped fighting.

"The good thing about Shiraishi is that we have that large swath of flat land that was reclaimed in the 1600s. Because of that we can plant vegetable gardens and dig wells. But on the other Kasaoka islands, there's just one mountain in the center and people live in the small strip of land around the perimeter. It's hard to have enough water then.

"I never worked, but I knew everything that was happening because I'd hear people talk. Many important people came to our house to talk to my husband. I'd serve tea, and I could always hear what they were saying, even when I tried hard not to."

The Imperial Palace

"Because of my husband's position, I've been to the Imperial Palace in Tokyo."

When I ask her to tell me about it, she says, "Empress Nagako, Hirohito's wife, was so beautiful! There was a big street and everyone was lined up, all kinds of people from all over Japan, and someone came over a mic and said, 'Attention, all attendees please look this way,' and the emperor appeared and greeted everyone with: 'I am Emperor Showa,' [she deepens her voice to mimic a baritone]. He walked down the path and every now and then would stop and talk to someone in the crowd standing along the road. He stopped very near us and he was so close we could hear his voice. I heard one person say to him 'I was so sorry to hear about that terrible incident you went through,' and just then a policeman appeared. I didn't understand what was meant by a 'terrible incident,' but Ryosaku told me later: during the previous New Year, as the year-end gifts arrived, a woman was opening one of the packages when it exploded and killed her. I'll never forget that kind man offering his condolences though. He expressed himself in a clear, beautiful voice. He was so compassionate.

"I've been to the Imperial Garden Party too! No one else on the island can say they've been invited to the emperor's garden party. It was held at the Asakasa Gyoen in Tokyo. There were so many cars, I thought we'd end up lost like the story of Urashima Taro.

"They wrote out an invitation for us in calligraphy. And we had to all wear kimonos with our family crests on the front and back. Our Harada family crest is a little different from other Haradas. The falcon feathers inside the circle are not quite the same.

"Whenever we'd go away from the island for a night, we'd send our luggage ahead by one week so when we arrived, it would already be there. At Asakasa Gyoen we had someone at the inn to assist us too. They announced, 'Mrs. Harada, the car has come.' When we came out of the inn and saw the car waiting for us, it was jet black with the imperial chrysanthemum crest on it! My husband had been to Asakasa Gyoen many times, but for me it was the first. And there were cars with gold emblems on them, VIPs, and policemen in uniforms with gold accessories, and they salute! I thought I was dreaming!

"I've always worn traditional Japanese clothes. Every now and then I wear a skirt, but my husband preferred me in a kimono. To the garden party I wore a formal *irotomesode* kimono. It was plum-pink, patterned on the hem only. Anyway, at the entrance to the garden, the first thing we saw was a pond. Once we were admitted inside, there were white tents lined up for miles. They were all food tents! Meat, sushi, udon, you name it—you could eat anything you wanted. My husband asked me what I'd like to eat but with a kimono on and the obi sash wrapped tight around my waist, I couldn't eat anything!

"So then someone on the hill spoke into a mic and said 'Everyone, look at the road, the emperor is about to appear.' They told everyone to line up to welcome him. The emperor looked so small in that big vast area. The Showa emperor, Hirohito, was bigger than his son Akihito—who became the Heisei emperor—and better looking. But even the Showa emperor looked small in that big space!

"Akihito's wife, the former empress Michiko, is pretty. She's kind of skinny but the Showa emperor's wife was plump and beautiful. The current empress, Masako-san, is cute. Now they have a child, Aiko-chan. I wonder if she'll be allowed to become empress. That would be nice, wouldn't it?"

The Widow Next Door

"My husband's aunt married someone on the next island, Takashima. He was serving on ships. He went into the war and was assigned to Hokkaido so they moved up there and he worked on a boat. But he was killed in the war. So young, not even old enough to have a child yet! His wife didn't like Hokkaido though, and said it was too cold. So eventually, Ryosaku went to Hokkaido and brought her back to Shiraishi. But she still needed some kind of income. Someone knew a woman who lived on the mainland who had farmland and lots of children. They needed a nanny. So Ryosaku took her over there and when she saw the place, she decided it would be okay and she lived there a long time helping out on the farm in addition to taking care of their children. Eventually, she came back here and lived by herself in that small house behind me, next to the hairdresser's shop.

"She was a nice old woman, and I took pity on her, so every morning I'd take over a pot of hot water for coffee. She used to tell me that although she didn't have any children, she felt she'd be okay because I was here.

"Well, one day I took over some food in the afternoon, and usually she would be very happy and say, 'Oh, what nice things you've brought me!' and open the door right away. But this time she didn't open the door even after I called out to her. I waited, but still no response. So I opened the door and went inside. I found her in the back room lying motionless on the floor. So I put the tray of food down, flew home and called Ryosaku's sister. We brought her back to my house and we gave her a funeral here. We had to because she didn't have any children to organize it for her. She was a nice woman. And her husband was on that transport ship and died in the war. So she was left alone. She never married again. She died at a good age though, anytime after eighty is pretty long."

Ghosts

When I ask her if she has any stories of growing up, she says, "I've seen ghosts three times!

"One day I was sitting on the wooden veranda of the house next to the Otafuku inn. It was nighttime and I was by myself, waiting for the fishermen to come back. Then, this large ball of fire appeared in the air and swept across in front of me. It wasn't a *hitodama* [a disembodied soul that looks like a fireball], it was much bigger, about a meter (3 feet) across. Then it blew over the mountain to the port area! I was very startled but I didn't dare tell anyone because I thought no one would ever believe me. But then I heard that others had seen it too! We never did figure out what that was.

"The second time was when I was in Okujo, where my house was, reading in my bed one night and I fell asleep. I woke up and thought I'd better turn out the light when I saw something outside the window. It was a fireball about as big as a head and it swept sideways and away between the two houses. I asked my grandmother and she said she saw it too, and that it was a hitodama! My childhood home was pretty near the cemetery, so it had to have been a hitodama. I wasn't scared though.

"The third time was when I had just moved into this house and went outside in the middle of the night to go to the outhouse. As I returned to the house, this perfectly round small red ball came flying through the air past me. It came from the direction of the cave above Shinmei Shrine. I asked my mother about it the next day and she said that if it's red and the size of a golf ball, then it's a *kami* [divine spirit]. 'You've seen a kami!' she said."

Life Begins at Sixty

"I had spent years taking care of my husband's mother. When she died, my husband said, 'You've worked so hard taking care of my mother, why don't you take the time and do something for yourself?' So with his permission, I started practicing gateball. We had lots of very good gateball players on Shiraishi then. I'd never played before even though all the others on the team had been playing a long time. But I was good! I became the champion of the entire Chugoku region! Oh, those were the days. We'd make bento-box lunches and go! I loved making myself bento lunches because I never had a chance to make them very much since I had no children.

"I wish my husband had gotten over his sickness. He died fifteen years ago when he was eighty years old. He was a good husband; always treated me well. I had lots of cousins and other relatives here on the island, but eventually everyone dies. So now I'm all alone and there's no one to take care of me or to inherit the property and house."

Three hours have passed and I regret that I must be on my way. She walks me back down the wooden hallway and we again pass the twelve-tatami-mat room. The shoji doors are still open and the hulking figure in the corner peers at us menacingly as we go by. "I find that samurai scary," she says of the lone Boys' Day decoration. "I don't like to look at it."

As I turn to leave through the door, she says, "You know that lady who lived in the house you moved into? She came to my old neighborhood after she married. She was a beautiful woman, cute and petite. She supported my husband when he was on the local council too. Her husband died in the war. She had a son but he moved away."

The Stone Bridge Lady stops to reflect. "I wonder why we had those wars. Really, we shouldn't go to war."

The Former Postmaster

A LONG GENTLE RAIN patters onto clay-tiled roofs, *sha-sha-sha*, as I walk down the road lined with Meiji-period houses. Spires of lavender reach out over the pathway, and cherry blossoms hang down from branches above and bobble in the breeze. When I arrive at the dwelling next to the post office, I close my umbrella and open the door.

"Sorry the two of us are old—we're not much good," says the Former Postmaster's wife as I enter their pristine house. Stepping up from the traditional *genkan* entrance hall into the tatami-mat living room I am surrounded by lush memorabilia—ornate hand-carved wooden statues, gold-framed certificates, and lengthy calligraphy scrolls, every artifact dusted and polished to gleaming. Soon they would introduce these items to me as if they were treasured members of their family.

Hung on the wall up near the ceiling to be nearer to the heavens, is a "god shelf," a staple in traditional Japanese homes. On the shelf rests a miniature wooden Shinto shrine flanked by porcelain vases that sprout *sakaki* branches considered sacred in the nature worship of Japan's indigenous religion. A dimple-skinned orange adds a touch of reverence, and color. "From long ago, whenever something bad happened we always made requests to the gods because we humans can't do everything on our own," says the Former Postmaster, who gives his age as ninety three and a half.

He points to the entrance hall I just stepped up from. "That used to be a dirt floor kitchen. We had a *kamado* stove there where we cooked rice then pounded it in a stone mortar.

"I was born at the very beginning of the Showa period. I have two brothers and five sisters; seven siblings in all. That was normal then. My father was a fisherman and my mother maintained the vegetable garden."

Tai-ami Fishing

The job of postmaster is usually an inherited one, handed down from father to son. But the Former Postmaster's father came from a lineage of fishermen. More than 350 years ago, at the beginning of the Edo period, fishermen in this area formed cooperatives to carry out *tai-ami*, a type of net fishing that involved more than fifty workers per catch. This area of the Inland Sea is especially good for trapping red snapper, called *tai* in Japanese.

The tai-ami method employs two large boats with twenty or so rowers on each, and about ten women who wait on the beach to help when the fish are brought back. A large net is stretched between the two tandem vessels forming a scoop which they could bring up from underneath. The men relied on their collective brawn to cinch up the net full of trapped fish. The sea area around Shiraishi is considered especially fertile. This abundance of fish is what kept the tai ami tradition fruitful for so long.

With the advent of motorized boats in the 1930s, tai-ami was replaced by *kinchaku-ami* (referring to the shape of the net: gathered at the top and pulled tight with a cord like a cotton coin purse).

"The way we fished was like this," the Former Postmaster explains. He puts the tips of both index fingers next to each other on the table, then drags each finger down in an arc on to show how each vessel created a half circle that joined up again at the 180-degree mark. "With engines, the boats could quickly surround a school of fish. Once the fish were entrapped, the men would heave the bulging net onto the deck."

The kinchaku-ami nets were shared among different groups of fishermen and this marked a very competitive and lively time—a golden era—of fishing. So successful were the Shiraishi fishermen they often appeared in newspapers in the 1950s showing off their record catches of *iriko*, small sardines (also called *niboshi*) used in the making the *dashi* base for Japanese soups and sauces.

"You know Takayama Mountain?" says the Former Postmaster. "A guy would stand on top of Takayama with a telescope looking for sardine pods." He gets to his feet and, like the child he was at the time, forms his two hands into a circle in front of one eye to create a make-believe telescope. "The fishermen were waiting on their boats below. From up there the watcher could look far out and see the movements of the fish. He was looking for a change in the color or surface of the water—a disturbance," he says, his eyes boring through the walls of his house towards the sea. "When the watcher spotted a school of fish, he'd pick up a pair of white flags, one in each hand, and signal to the boats by waving the flags." He shoots his hands above his head, holding imaginary flags, and leans to one side while yelling, "To the left!" He thrusts his arms up again in a semaphoric gesture. "To the right!" he hollers. "And the chase would begin as the boats headed to that area."

The silvery iriko were transferred from the net, flopping and shimmering in the sunlight, into round wooden casks, then passed to a smaller third boat to be shuttled back to shore while the huntsmen continued fishing.

Each house was awarded a portion of fish based on how many people they had helping with the catch. "My family always received six barrels," he tells me, rather proudly. "Yes, six. I know because when I was a kid, I used to go out and help."

In those days, they fished for *sawara* (a type of mackerel), red snapper, pufferfish, squid, and thread-sail filefish.

"Did you fish in the wintertime?" I ask.

"Yes, and when it was cold we wore *donza*," he says, referring to the local name for padded fishing jackets. When one is brought out to show me I marvel at the thickness of these handmade fishermen's coats sewn with layers of cloth.

"They didn't have rubber boots then either, so they fished either barefoot or in straw sandals, or *tabi* [split-toed socks]," he says.

The Post Office

"I inherited the post office position from my father's older brother. He had no children to hand the job down to, so they adopted me into their family. That original wooden post office next door to us was built in Showa 4 [1929]. The new modern one across the street was built in Heisei 6 [1994].

"I was the postmaster for thirty-three years. If you include the telephone work I did in Okayama when I first got out of school—because in those days the telephone and mails were the same office—that's seventy-something years! That's why I received that certificate from the emperor," he says, pointing to the gilt-framed calligraphic artwork stamped with the imperial crest. "It's for my long service."

His wife, who disappeared during the fishing story, reemerges with iced tea and *senbei* rice crackers which she places on the low table between us where we sat on the tatami-mat floor. "He worked so hard," she says. "He received a certificate from the temple priest too. See? This is from Kairyuji Temple. This one over here is from the Red Cross. He's done a lot of things in different places. Even though he can't go places to help these days because he's too old, he sends money."

"We had six years of elementary school" says the Former Postmaster, "then two years of junior high on the island, then, if we wanted to go to high school, we had to go to Kasaoka on the mainland. I lived in a dormitory there so I could continue school. Some of us went from junior high straight into work while other kids went on to technical high school.

"Then in my second year of high school, the war started." He pauses for a moment and swallows hard. "Classes were interrupted because students had to go work in factories for the war effort. I commuted from my school to a factory in Mizushima, just across the sea from here, where I worked making airplane wings. Then in June, after the Americans entered the war, the Mizushima factory was bombed. On the day of the bombing, I was on my way back to Shiraishi for a visit, so I just missed it. But I could hear the planes—*do-do-don, do-do-don*—going over Mizushima. At the time I had no idea what was happening.

"Until I could go back to school, I dabbled in different things. First I worked at the NTT telephone company in Okayama. I used to go out at night and I learned a bit about life. After that they sent me to Tokyo to study communications management for post, telegrams, and telephone. But in Showa 32 [1957] I returned to Shiraishi to become the head of the island post office."

His wife says, "After junior high on Shiraishi, I went to high school in Kasaoka. I returned to Shiraishi in Showa 32 and got a job at the post office. That's where we met. We married the next year."

"It was really nice to get a wife so young!" her husband butts in with a smile.

"I was born in Showa 11 [1936]," she says.

"On April 5!" her husband adds.

At that time, all mail for Shiraishi was routed through Kitagi Island next door, where it was sorted first. "We had to take a boat to Kitagi to get the mail, whatever the weather—rain, wind, typhoons. That was difficult and we had to use our own boat. We mostly delivered letters and small packages. In those days everyone wrote letters."

"Because we didn't have telephones!" his wife interjects.

"Well, there were telephones but most people didn't have them," he clarifies. "If you were in a hurry, you sent a telegram. I also stayed overnight at the post office at times to receive incoming telegrams."

"That's right," she confirms. "We had to deal with both telegrams and telephones. When the telegrams came in we'd head over the mountain to deliver them."

"When I first became postmaster there were only seventeen telephone numbers on the island for 2,300 people. Then the dentist got a line so we had eighteen."

"Before that, only the village hall, the doctor, the shops, the rock quarries and inns had telephones," says his wife. "The stone companies took their orders by telegram, so we had to take the orders over to the back of the island. We had to live right next door to the post office so we were always on hand to make the deliveries."

The Former Postmaster continues. "There was a main mountain path but we also used the pilgrimage path."

I'm surprised to learn that the island's three-hundred-and-fifty-year-old pilgrimage path was once a postman's delivery route. One of my favorite walks, the path is imbued with abundant seasonal wildflowers and is punctuated with tawny boulders that shelter small stone Buddhist statues. Following this high road to the headland, you must be careful not to stumble, or you'll topple straight down through the forest of skinny tree legs into the maw of the rocky shore below. The path continues to the headland, past the lobster-claw jetties marking the port entrance, and at last delivers you to a strand of beach at the bottom of a wood, where a cluster of four wooden houses, struggling under heavy clay-tiled roofs, is protected by a seawall. The casual observer would find this to be the end of the path, and, after turning to face the sea to watch a passing ferry or two, would soon retrace their steps back to the port. But a local, especially at the spring or autumn equinox, might slip through a small bamboo-grass opening, perceived only by the trained eye, and proceed straight into the thick brush. Once through the thick bamboo grass, the forest opens up and he—or more often, she—continues along the pilgrimage path that hugs the seashore. She'll pay her respects to more small stone Buddhist deities by leaving offerings of green-leafed *shikibi* branches in the vase provided while praying to her ancestors. If she completes the circuit of all eighty-eight deities, she will have traveled the 6-mile (10-kilometer) circumference of the island. In the past it could be done in a day, but now it takes two, because the pilgrimage trail is not so well worn nor marked, and one easily wanders along lost.

"Now you can't see the path for all the weeds!" says the Former Postmaster. "But in the old days, the islanders would walk the pilgrimage and pray at the spring equinox. Also, we had lots of pilgrims come to the temple on Shiraishi. There weren't enough inns for them to stay at. But after the war, the nearby castle town of Fukuyama on the mainland became more popular for sightseeing."

When I ask if they have any special memories from that time, the wife says, "We have no interesting stories. We worked too hard to do anything else!" Her husband is pensive for a moment before remarking, "We've had a lot of nice things done for us."

"All he has done is work his whole life!" she says with a chortle. "But he came down with stomach cancer when he was eighty-eight and he lost a lot of weight. He reached a low of 47 kilos [about 100 pounds]. He's back up to 50 kilos now but he's not that strong anymore. Until he was eighty-eight he was very healthy, and he did everything for me."

"We have two children and two grandchildren. All boys. One is in Tokyo. He won't come back. The other comes back occasionally to visit. Everyone moves so far away these days. It's lonely," admits the Former Postmaster.

"Even where you live Amy, the lady died a long time ago. The son doesn't come back," notes his wife. "Back when we were young, your house wasn't there."

She sweeps a hand toward the veritable museum of artifacts and family memorabilia. "All this was passed down to us because my husband's oldest brother didn't have any children. So we inherited everything. Everyone thinks they want to preserve the old things, but we're too elderly to worry about preserving anything. And no one else is here to carry it on."

I want to linger to ponder that statement, but my silence is interrupted by a rumbling noise from the road outside. A shadow passes the window, and I recognize the outline of a dump truck that has recently been groaning up and down the lane, ferrying mounds of dirt and leaving ribbons of muddy tire streaks behind. The modern behemoth is squeezing itself down the narrow road made long before cars ever existed, long before telephones or electricity poles, and long before anyone considered that the graves on Tomiyama Hill could plummet down the mountainside during a typhoon and need to be hauled away.

Barely able to hear anymore for the roar of the truck outside, I thank the Former Postmaster and his wife for their time.

The Fish Trapper's Father

THE PORT is the hub of life on any small Japanese island. The hustle and bustle of ferry boats entering and exiting, passengers embarking and disembarking, and goods being delivered and distributed is what distinguishes an island from an equally small countryside village on the mainland. The port exudes safety and familiarity; it is synonymous with home. It is the port to which the fishermen return from the sea with their catches, and the port from which relatives living far away are met and welcomed back home for the holidays by their loved ones.

The Shiraishi port was constructed from 1682 to 1691 during Japan's feudal period. As six tombs here from the Kofun period (300–538 AD) indicate, Shiraishi Island was inhabited long before the construction of the port, but the island wasn't fully developed until the daimyo lord of Fukuyama Castle on the mainland nearby decided to appropriate this land to graze his military horses.

Before stone blocks were used to reinforce and sculpt the harbor into a traditional U-shape, the area was a natural inlet, stretching 50 acres (20 hectares) into the interior of the island, almost splitting it in half. Shallow and tidal, one could walk across this stretch of water at certain times of the day when the tide had receded. After the construction of the port, the empty 50 acres (20 hectares) of tidal area was converted to pastureland. This project was started in 1694, the same year the poet Matsuo Basho died, and construction finished in 1701. This second stage included a breakwater between the pastureland and the port.

It is around this port that the Fish Trapper and his father, Danshi, have worked their whole lives.

It's just after seven in the morning when I hear an electric cart purr up to the back of my house. From my kitchen window I can see Danshi-san's cropped hair, his square frame hoisting shoulders like a football player's. He moves calculatingly on his pins, easing his way to my door. As I let him in, I notice how long and narrow his nose is, and how when he smiles, his mouth draws up on either side like the flutes of an anchor. His hair is the white wake of a wave, and his eyes sparkle like the first rays of the morning sun on the ripples of an incoming tide. There's plenty of life left in this ninety-five-year-old.

Danshi is hard of hearing, but none of the elderly around here wear a hearing aid. I lift my voice a few octaves, repeat my phrases, and he somehow navigates my foreign accent well enough to answer my questions. He takes a sip of coffee before starting his story.

"I was born in Taisho 15 [1926], on February 22. My father was a fisherman too. He was born in Meiji 16 [1883] and fought in the Russo-Japanese War. My grandfather fished also, so I'm the third generation fisherman and my son is fourth. I have three children, two girls and one boy. My wife died just last November. My son's wife makes all the meals at home. We eat mostly fish."

"How many grandchildren do you have?" I ask.

"I have three."

"Only three?"

"I have three inside grandchildren and six outside grandchildren, so nine altogether," he says referring to the different terminology used for counting grandchildren depending on whether they belong to one's son or one's daughter. Since men stay with their family, their children are called *uchimago* (inside grandchildren). Since daughters leave the clan to marry into other households, their children are called *sotomago* (outside grandchildren).

School Days

"The only classmates left from my year are the Stone Bridge Lady and Katsuko [the Pufferfish Widow].

"I'm trying to think of what we wore to school then. I don't think we had uniforms at that time. The boys wore regular clothes to school as far as I remember, but most of the girls wore kimonos. In those days we made our own sandals with braided bamboo leaves and rubber from bicycle tires. But at school we had to leave our footwear at the door and put on straw sandals inside the building, so there was straw dust all over the place!"

The old wooden school he is referring to was in use up until about twenty years ago. I still remember standing with the other islanders watching the flames leap out of the old building. Even though I'd never had much to do with the school, I was moved by the bewitching power of the fire and the furious and unforgiving blaze. "Such a shame!" people gasped. We were cordoned off from the controlled blaze, perhaps so no one would try to rescue their childhood memories as they watched them morph into black curls of smoke, cremating the past. Even the fire truck was eerily stationary as if watching time burn away.

Adults, mainly officials from the mainland who had never attended the school, decided to raze the structure as a new concrete monstrosity of a school had recently been built, making the old wooden school redundant. While the gymnasium was repurposed into a hall for traditional weaving, the other buildings were kindled to soot.

This event saddened the islanders, who had gathered on this evening to give their school a proper farewell. To this day, there has been nothing built in that spot. One hundred years of history, replaced by a vacant field of rampant, untamed weeds.

"After elementary school, I went to the junior high here, which was two years. We didn't have to go though. They weren't very strict about attendance. But I went. I had seventy people in my class in elementary school. It's hard to believe we don't have any students in the elementary school at all now and just two in junior high.

"It was hard to keep warm in winter back then. We'd light the *hibachi* brazier. We didn't have a *kotatsu* heated table. At night it was pretty cold in the futon. During the day, we made bonfires outside in the garden to keep warm."

Traditional Japanese houses, with their paper doors and open verandas, are designed to be cool in the summer, which means they're also not very cozy in winter. In milder climates of the Inland Sea, the inside of the house is cooler than the outside, even in the wintertime. There are still people here who sit outside on the wooden veranda around a small bonfire in the garden in the wintertime.

"We burned pine needles for fuel to heat the bath but there are few pine trees now. Before your house was built, there were large black pines and red pines all up and down the harbor. When we were kids we used to climb out on the branches and jump into the sea during high tide. There was one particular tree that faced at an angle to the west, and it was the best one."

When I ask him what his best memories are about his school days, he pauses for a moment before his long face widens at the bottom into a large grin. He chuckles the way one does when thinking about something in the past that seems so far away it's irretrievable. "Well, when I was young, we didn't have any entertainment like television or such, so we'd go night crawling," he says, referring to a practice called *yobai*, where boys snuck into girls' houses at night to fool around. "At around nine or ten o'clock, we'd go over to our classmates' houses."

The girls would leave the doors of the house open for them and the boys would crawl into their futons. Often, they stayed long into the night.

World War II

"When I was eighteen, I got a red envelope in the mail. I knew it meant I was drafted into the military. It was in May, Showa 19 [1944]. Three other guys and I took the tests to become servicemen. The other two made the top grade, Class A, in the physical-ability test, so they went to the front lines. But I failed, so I was assigned to work on boat engines. The boat I was on was near the base in Wakayama. That boat was old, not one of the new ones specially procured for the war. We took it to Tokushima to have it fixed. While we were there, another guy took over my job and I was put on a different boat. It was good timing because that old boat got fired on by machine guns and that guy was killed. The entire boat was burned. Those who did survive received medals of honor from the emperor. And you know what? The other two friends of mine who made the top grade in the physical ability test—they also died.

"When I came back after the war ended, I helped my parents with their fishing business. I was just visiting when I came back but when I saw that my father could make 100,000 yen in a twenty-four-hour period by fishing all day and all night, I decided to stay and become a fisherman. At that time, we did *kinchaku-ami* net fishing. One barrel of baby shrimp brought in 20,000 to 40,000 yen.

"My son catches small shrimp, Japanese sea bass and tiny fish called *ami*. We don't fish *iriko* sardines anymore because you need a lot of people for that. We have so few fishermen now. In my time, there were about twenty boats at one pier. The port used to be a very busy place and it was really noisy when all us fishermen came back at two or three in the morning. The wives would meet their husbands with their catches and sort the fish according to type, ice them down in wooden boxes, and load the boxes onto the *namasen*, the boat that takes them to the fish markets in Kasaoka City to sell.

"I really liked being a fisherman. I still repair the nets just for a bit of pocket money."

I ask if he knew Eiko, who used to live here, but all he says is, "I remember they had a small boat they used for fishing."

He gets up to leave, and I help him to the door.

A Reluctant Innkeeper

LIGHT AND DAINTY, Tetsumi flits over to the entrance of the inn with arms pressed down at her sides and hands jutting out like little wings. Wearing a simple button-down blouse and gingham pants, she bends at the waist in a deep Japanese bow. Of course, I don't warrant such a deep and respectful bow but Tetsumi treats all people this way, as if they are esteemed guests of the upper echelons of society.

I don't know Tetsumi well, so rather than just showing up on her doorstep, I made an appointment through her daughter-in-law the last time I was at the grocery store. "Sure," Keiko had said, while tallying up my apple and yogurt at the register. "But you better book in quick because the summer starts soon and she'll be too busy after that." Keiko made a quick call on her cellphone pressing her chin to her right shoulder to secure it while giving me my change with both hands. Then she gave a nod and said, "How about tomorrow?"

And here I am, standing in the hallway of the Otafuku inn, being welcomed by the gracious septuagenarian whose Japanese is so polite it pours from her geranium red lips like treacle off a honey dipper.

She leads me in and sits me down at the table in front of the window where a rugose pine tree stretches a lazy arm across the windowpane. Tetsumi alights on the chair opposite me.

A woman smocked in Hello Kitty brings iced coffee and cheesecake on a tray and sets it down in front of us. Then with perfect posture, hands gently folded on her lap, Tetsumi starts speaking in her melodious voice.

Childhood

"So let me start with the grocery store. My father worked on the next island to the west at a company called Konoshima Kagaku where he

48

washed crane machinery. My mother tilled the vegetable gardens with my grandmother here at home. Those who weren't married yet, and children like me who were still in elementary school in the 1950s, helped out in the gardens. We also were in charge of carrying buckets of sludge from the toilets to fertilize the gardens.

"Everyone grew vegetables back then, mostly wheat and potatoes, because we could sell those things for cash to the JA [Japan Agricultural co-operative]. Rice was distributed by the government, even rice not grown in Japan. But there was never enough rice. We ate an awful lot of wheat and potatoes," she says, laughing while covering her mouth with her cupped hand.

"I was one of five kids, so I had to help my parents. At that time we needed to heat the bath water with fuel, so we children would scour the mountain areas and bundle up pine needles in bags which we carried over our shoulders. We never had enough fuel, so even if there was just a tiny breeze we'd rush out to the mountain and collect any fallen needles. You had to get out there early before anyone else!

"We had enough water for our daily living because we had a well that we pumped by hand. But we still had to carry the buckets of water from the well to the bath. Those who didn't have wells had to ask their neighbors to let them use their bath. Of course, no one had much money, so rather than paying, they might take some wheat, or fuel. We didn't share our bath often because we already had a pretty big family.

"People just helped each other in those days. We were busy every day just surviving.

"We didn't have money to go on to higher education from high school, so as soon as I graduated I went to Osaka. I owned hardly anything. I remember I left with just one bag with all my belongings in it.

"For two years I was an office lady. It was so much fun! When I was in Osaka I was free and I could do whatever I wanted whenever I pleased. I lived in my uncle's house so I didn't have to pay rent. I hardly made any money, but life was great. I was young. Even without money we went to many places and still enjoyed ourselves."

Arranged Marriage

"Then my parents called me back to the island. They wanted me to get married and they had set up everything. Back here, I felt like I'd fallen into Hell. I was only twenty when I married and it changed my life completely. I had to get up in the wee hours of every morning to make tofu and then work at the grocery store till late at night. Then from nine at night I had to prepare the bath for all the family members and do the laundry. Then we'd all get up in the morning and make tofu again.

"My husband's parents were very strict. My husband's father was in the Japanese police force, and they had been transferred to China during the Great East Asian War to help out with law enforcement. At the end of World War II, they were repatriated from China but when they came back they had absolutely nothing but the clothes on their backs. Having been gone from the island so long, they didn't even own a vegetable plot anymore so they had no food to eat."

Even a year after Japan's surrender, over two million Japanese had yet to be repatriated from former overseas colonies. Many died in the war's aftermath due to outbreaks of disease such as smallpox, typhus, and cholera. Some perished while en route to Japan. They were only allowed to bring back with them what they could carry and were subject to further delays due to medical examinations and quarantines. Some even left newborns behind, an estimated three thousand such children, fearing they would never make the extended journey back to Japan and thus had a better chance of surviving by staying behind.

"There were many horror stories about Japanese who were sent to China. Some died because of the horrific conditions. I heard of one woman who was on a train that was held up because a railway bridge had been bombed. During the delay she gave birth right there on the train! So I know that my husband's parents really lived through difficult times.

"To support themselves, my in-laws started making tofu here on the island, waking up at two o'clock in the morning to make it then selling it door to door. This was before I married into the family. At that time, the island didn't have paved roads like now so they carried the tofu on bamboo poles over their shoulders over the narrow mountain paths. They walked all over the island of course, but in those days rock quarrying was going strong on the back side of the island, so they sold a lot of tofu to the workers over there at lunchtime. After a while it took a toll on their health. So they decided to look for an easier job. There were boats from Kobe and Osaka delivering goods up and down the Seto Inland Sea and they managed to get jobs on the boats. But the person who arranged the work for them took most of the money. They had been tricked, and accumulated a lot of debt.

"My mother-in-law's side of the family had an extra house on the island so they started a grocery store there in 1954. I started working there as soon as I married into the family. At that time soy sauce, vinegar, and miso were weighed and charged per gram, so you only bought as much as you needed that day. In those days people didn't have much purchasing power. The variety of goods was paltry so most people lived very simply on fried food, tofu and *konnyaku* which they bought and took home in their own containers. We didn't have any luxury foods nor many sweets. Even *senbei* rice crackers were sold one by one. The store was open until nine at night and until ten during the summer Bon festival when everyone comes back from the cities to visit their families. We had very little free time.

"Everything was brought over from the markets in Kasaoka. There was a middleman who worked with wholesalers and retail shops and would send the goods over on the ferry. We'd go and pick up the goods at the port in a *riyaka* hand cart and bring them back to the store.

"There were quite a few fish stalls around the island at that time too. You know the area where the graves fell off the edge of the ridge during the typhoon last year? Right where the road gets a little bigger? That's where the fish stalls were lined up. Nowadays there are none left.

"But just after we were married, my mother-in-law died and my father-in-law immediately remarried a woman who didn't lift a finger to help. So I was the one who had to do everything. They yelled at me all the time. After three months I lost 10 kilos [22 pounds]! It was because of fear. They were always yelling at me. I never understood why. I became pregnant right away too.

"My in-laws never helped me at home nor with the shop. I did it all, including cooking meals and preparing the bath. I tried my best to do it diligently and pleasantly. What it amounts to is that my husband's father and his new wife thought they were too good for this kind of work and I became their servant.

"But that's how the times were and there was nothing I could do about it. Nowadays, women don't put up with this kind of treatment. If I were a little smarter, I wouldn't have either. But once you have children, you can't leave. So, that's just how I lived," she said sighing through a jeweled smile.

Becoming an Innkeeper

"Long ago there were no inns on the island. Travelers had to ask to stay at the temple. In those days we also had a lot of people come to see the lanterns set off on the sea at the end of the Bon festival. They wanted to stay overnight, so we would rent out a room or two in our house to such people. We didn't serve any food but there were places they could get something basic to eat.

"You know the barber? His oldest son started the Otafuku inn, and his wife was my aunt. They didn't have any children themselves, so they adopted my male cousin into their family to carry on the line. But he started a different inn and called it the Otafuku Bekkan.

"Eventually more inns were built. The 60s and 70s were the most prosperous time here and little by little the food became fancier. In those days the inn was busy even in the wintertime. Most people from the mainland wanted to eat fresh fish from the Inland Sea, and we had some excellent winter fish. Groups came out for end of year parties and beginning of the year parties and they'd stay overnight. The staff wore kimonos and sang *enka* traditional songs. It was a lively time. My uncle continued to expand the Otafuku, eventually ending up with twenty rooms. He also built a rock bath on the second floor.

"They didn't serve meat in those days, just sushi. Nowadays people want more meat than fish. We even serve dessert!

"And there were no swimming pools then either, so everyone came to the sea to swim. Nowadays, even schools have their own pools.

"So anyway, my aunt and uncle were living here at the inn but eventually with the continued decline in numbers of customers, they couldn't cover the expenses to manage it and they didn't have the strength to do all the work anymore. So, when I was fifty-eight and it was time to retire from the grocery store, I came here. My husband, together with my son and his wife, take care of the store now. The inn is a lot of work though, and we don't make enough money to feel it's worthwhile. Even if we had more customers, we'd have to knock them back because we don't have enough staff. So I'm not sure what will happen. I'm already seventy-four.

"Life is better now than when I was a child, but there were good things about those times too. It's true we wore dirty clothes and didn't own any new clothes to change into. We had lice in our hair but we picked them out of each other's heads for amusement. We didn't have toys to play with so we entertained ourselves with games like *ishi koroke* with stones and we played *oni gokko* tag. But whatever we did we made a lively time of it.

"My grandkids don't seem to have as much fun, just staring into smartphones all day long. I know times change, but I wonder how much fun that can be."

The Pufferfish Widow
and Yakutoshi

"I'M NINETY-FIVE YEARS OLD!" crows Katsuko. Then she droops her shoulders, rounds her back, and deflates a little. "I was born in the Taisho era. *Maa*, it was a short era that ended after only fifteen years. I was born one year before the end, in Taisho 14 [1925]." Katsuko uses the word *maa* the way English speakers use "Well . . . "

The short Taisho era was a time of peace before the build-up to World War II. The Japanese invaded Manchuria in 1931 and the second Sino-Japanese War took place in 1937, leading to the Pacific War which, with the entry of the Americans, would become World War II. Katsuko's own lifetime has spanned four Japanese eras (and emperors): Taisho, 1912–1926 (Yoshihito); Showa, 1926–1989 (Hirohito); Heisei, 1989–2019 (Akihito); and the current Reiwa (Naruhito).

This woman strutted over to the beach area under a beating sun to chat with me. She presented herself in a brilliant white, cleanly pressed smock as if she were showing up for a shift with the kitchen crew of a cruise liner. Her son accompanied her and the three of us are sitting at a table in the shade of a pawlounia tree across the road from the beach.

"I have two children. This is my oldest son," she tells me in a slightly gravelly voice while indicating the sixty-one-year-old sitting next to her. I know her son, Yakutoshi, because he works part-time at the ferry ticket office. "My daughter died four years ago."

When I ask her what life was like on the island when she was young, she tells me "I had seventy other students in my class in elementary school and we were all in that old wooden school house."

"She was the best student in her class and was good at calligraphy writing," interjects Yakutoshi. During his mother's time, writing was a highly prized skill among the common people. "She wrote letters to the soldiers who had gone off to fight in the war and encouraged them to do their best. But when she was in her first year of junior high, she had to quit to take care of her younger brothers and sisters."

U-Turn

Yakutoshi is part of the *yutaan* (U-Turn) movement, referring to those who leave the island after graduating from school, take jobs on the mainland for many years, then move back to retire where they grew up, and where their parents lived and worked their whole lives. "I moved back to the island to take care of my mother, but she's the one looking after me!" he claims.

"I worked at that steel factory over there until I retired," he says, looking over at the simmering black smoke rising from the tall flutes of the factory complex five miles across the water on the mainland.

The Inland Sea is dotted with dozens of coastal factories. The most efficient form of transporting cargo is by ship, even more so since the country's highways are narrow and crowded. All day long, large ships pass in and out of coastal ports, loading and unloading everything from raw steel on spools to assembled motor cars. The larger ships head out of the Inland Sea to deliver Japanese goods all over the world and to return laden with consumables from China and other countries. On windy days, the smog around the formidable factory across the water is temporarily lifted, only to reveal soot-stained buildings in a smudged charcoal landscape. At nighttime the skies are brightened from flames that rocket straight up as they burn the coke ovens.

Katsuko was thirty-three years old when she gave birth to Yakutoshi on Shiraishi Island. She was really only thirty-two (her birthday falls on September 1) but the Japanese custom at that time was that all citizens turned a year older on New Year's Day, no matter when their birthday. Women were thought to be especially prone to misfortune in the years when they turn nineteen, thirty-three, and thirty-seven. These bad-luck years are called *yakudoshi*. For men, the yakudoshi years are twenty-five, forty-two, sixty-one, and the ages for both sexes can vary slightly depending on the region. In Katsuko's day, people were far more superstitious than they are now, so this fear of bad luck encouraged women to discard babies born in a mother's bad-luck year. Women feared that if they kept a child born in their thirty-third year, the Shinto gods might impose their wrath upon the family.

On Shiraishi, the mothers worked out a system they felt would be fair enough to deflect bad luck and still allow them to keep their newborns. A mother would indeed "throw out the child" by placing the infant on its back in a culvert of water between the rice fields. An elderly matron of the village, however, would be on standby to scoop up the newborn and return it to the mother telling her the baby now had renewed strength and thus, should be kept.

"But, maa, when my son was born, I thought he looked like a strong baby already," Katsuko said defiantly. "So I kept him. And I named him Yakutoshi."

Yakutoshi is not a typical Japanese name; the mother used a play on words for the bad-luck year in hopes of dispelling any ill fortune.

"People are surprised when they hear my unusual name but when I tell them the reason, they understand," says Yakutoshi.

"I was twenty-five when I married," says Katsuko. "Most women were married by twenty, but the Pacific War was on when I was that age. With so many men off fighting, there were fewer around to marry." Katsuko had to wait her turn.

"I was one of seven children, and I married the boy next door—maa, there was one house between us," she corrects herself.

"We held the wedding ceremony at the house. I grew up wearing kimonos, but they were threadbare because we wore the same one every day. Since I didn't have a wedding kimono, I just wore the best one I had, which was the silk one I wore at the New Year." Some Japanese children received new kimonos every New Year, but Katsuko didn't.

"For five years after I was married, I couldn't get pregnant, so I went for moxibustion treatments in Kasaoka. Then I got pregnant the next year and had a girl. When I had my daughter, I gave birth at home. The doctor lived just a few doors away, so when I was ready they just told him 'Come quick, come quick!'

"The year after that I had Yakutoshi. Maa, I didn't have a mother-in-law to help me, so I thought two children was enough. Then I went and had moxibustion again so I wouldn't get pregnant."

Island Adoption

There were two adoption systems on the island then. One was called *yoshien-gumi* for families that didn't have a male heir to inherit their business and property, or for those bereft of a female child. In such cases, families would adopt either a relative such as a niece or nephew, or a child from a different family. These children would live with the adoptive parents and change their names to theirs because the intention was for them to become an heir.

The other system, called *fude no oya* (literally "ink brush parent") was particular to this island. These children had no obligation to, nor inheritance from the adoptive family and they didn't usually move to the family's house. The "parents" of fude no oya, however, were responsible for helping the child out, such as with school supplies, looking after them if they got into trouble or if their real parents couldn't provide for them. The adoptive parents served another important role too: to help find a marriage partner for them if asked.

Wealthy individuals on the island often had many fude no oya children because numerous families asked them to take their child in such a relationship. The island doctor is said to have had ten. Although parents of both parties decided who would be adopted into which family, the process didn't start until the child was in junior high school and the adoptee was in charge of taking the ultimate step. If the child was female, she would prepare a gift of a folding fan inside a fancy box to give to her prospective family. A boy would take a two-liter bottle of sake. The bottle neck was bound with string made from kombu seaweed and two auspicious dried *niboshi* fish were twisted into the fibers. Instead of the parents accompanying the child to the other house, a friend would take them. Upon arrival at the home, the friend would announce, "I have brought your son," or "I have brought your daughter." They would be invited inside, the gift presented, and they would celebrate with tea and snacks. After a short chat with the family, the relationship was sealed and the child and his companion would return home.

"You know old Mikizo-san?" says Yakutoshi. "He passed away a couple years ago, but when he was still in high school he came to our house with a bottle of sake, and my family adopted him. When the time came for him to get married, he also asked us to find him a wife."

Father Was a Fisherman

"My father was a fisherman. He's famous for how he died," says Yakutoshi with a token laugh. It's not unusual for Japanese people to smile or give an uncomfortable laugh in these situations. "Have you heard the story?" he asks me.

I haven't.

"Well, first let me give you some background, then I'll get into that. In the 1930s, engines came into use on boats, so by that time my father was fishing on motorized wooden boats. The carpenters made the boats in front of your house, Amy, where the Fishermen's Union is. They'd have a *mochinage* rice-cake-throwing ceremony from the deck of a new boat to christen the vessel, then everyone would go to Kompirasan, the local shrine for fishermen, to pray. There, I remember the Shinto priest would bless the offerings with a sword."

"My husband did *kinchaku-ami* net fishing for twenty years," interrupts his mother. "There used to be lots of fishers' sheds on the beach. There were about three people in each shed and they'd boil up the *iriko* fish in vats."

Katsuko and the other women ferried the iriko from the boats up to the fishing shacks that stippled the length of the beach. "We carried the fish in big wooden *taru* barrels. Boy, they were heavy! They were loaded with so many fish, I always wished there were more people to help carry. They weighed about 50 kilos [110 pounds] each and it took two people to carry one between us on our shoulders. One day the storehouse caught fire and the barrels all burned. I was so happy!"

In the fishing shacks, after they boiled up the fish, they'd lay them out in the sun to dry. "The whole beach would be full of straw mats. Maa, if it was raining though, the fisherman couldn't go out because the fish would start rotting before they could dry out." The dried iriko were put into paper bags, tied up and taken to be sold on the mainland in Kasaoka City.

Yakutoshi elaborates. "They caught the iriko and other small fish using nets with tiny holes. They'd go out fishing at night, take a bento lunch with them to eat, and return in the morning. Then they'd go back out again during the day. These days fishermen only go out once, but at the time my parents were newly married, they were poor, so they fished all day and all night to make enough money to get by."

"Maa, I was always working so hard, I never had time to leave the island or go anywhere else," says Katsuko. "But we ate sashimi every day. We also cooked vegetables we grew ourselves like shallots and cabbage. We had a tree of small peaches. Figs too. No matter how much work we put into the figs, they'd be rotten inside, because this kid here didn't prune the tree properly!"

Yakutoshi gets back to the original story. "When I was a first year junior high school student my father suddenly died. He was eating sashimi and he felt his mouth get tingly. He knew exactly what had happened but it was already too late. He had eaten the poisonous part of a *fugu* pufferfish. Everyone knows me as the boy whose father died from eating fugu. It was a huge funeral. We just recently held the fifty-year Buddhist memorial ceremony of his death."

"After my Yoichi died," says Katsuko, "I went to work at the Otafuku inn as a *nakaisan* [female staff member] until I was seventy-two. During the day we wore *mompe* pants or a skirt. But at night we had to entertain, so we changed into kimonos. There were lots of guests then. Before people left in the evening, they'd all put together a tip for me."

"She'd make seven or eight thousand yen a day in tips!" her son interjects.

"That was back when Shiraishi was getting popular. All I had to do was go to work and I'd come home with a pocketful of money. In those days, we had guests year-round. We were busy all the time. There used to be a lot more people living on the island then too.

"You live in Eiko's house, don't you, Amy?" Katsuko says, as I'm wrapping up the interview. "My husband's brother was Eiko's husband. But he went off to war right after he married, and died within the first year. That was before I married into the family, so I didn't know him."

The Outsider

THE PREVIOUS *okami* (female manager) of the Nakanishiya *ryokan* inn is perhaps the best-known woman on the island. The Nakanishiya has been operating since before World War II, but the rules for operating Japanese inns changed after the war. Mama-san, as everyone calls her, is said to have received official permission needed to run the inn directly from General MacArthur, the commander of the US occupying forces in Japan from 1945 to 1952.

Mama-san is known for having run the inn with an iron fist and for even doing most of the cooking herself. "Even if there were a hundred guests, I did the cooking for all of them," she once told me.

"One time when I went over to help out," remembered a neighbor, "some esteemed guests arrived and insisted on being greeted by the okami-san. So I called back to the kitchen to Mama-san. When she came out, the guests were so surprised to see she was completely covered in fish guts!"

I approached her son for an introduction to his mother, since the closest I'd ever come to seeing her was through the picture window of her house, which faces the beach. The son kept agreeing to do so, but with no results. This is when I realized that relations weren't that smooth between family members. So today, I've taken it upon myself to go to her house and introduce myself. She welcomes me with the brightest smile. Before I even have a chance to ask her any questions, she launches into her personal history.

"I was born on Kitagi Island next door and my father was wealthy. Kitagi is big, so it had four separate villages, each with its own village headman. We never did anything together as an island the way they do here on Shiraishi. We acted as four independent neighborhoods with our own festivals, schools, and events. I lived in the Toyoura neighborhood, where our house and land was. There were seven children in my family and I'm the youngest. I'm eighty-eight and three of my siblings are still living. Only one is still on Kitagi though.

"When I was a child, I didn't have to work like other children did. Even as an adult, I've never received a salary envelope from a job. We didn't always have a lot of food, but we had rice and wheat because we grew our own crops. We owned a lot of land too: houses, garden plots, some on the mountain. My brothers went on to college after high school. Then, when I was twenty, I had an arranged marriage and came to Shiraishi. I married my husband here in Showa 28 [1953] on October 10. Since it was still just eight years after the end of the war, we didn't have a big wedding ceremony as it was considered rude to show your wealth in front of so many people who didn't have anything.

"When I came over from Kitagi for my wedding, I wore a kimono of course, with *geta* clog sandals. We loaded my wedding trousseau, inside a large wooden trunk, onto the boat. Everyone saw me off from the port on Kitagi and waved goodbye. When I arrived on Shiraishi there was a welcome procession to take me to the Nakanishiya, the inn my husband's parents owned. We walked from the port through the interior of the village and everyone came out of their houses to see me. The wooden trunk was so heavy it was lassoed to a bamboo pole so two men could shoulder it, one guy in front of the trunk and one in back. People lined the road all the way to the beach near the inn. In those days, it was the custom for the bride to open the chest and show everyone her fine kimonos and accessories. So everyone came to have a gander!

"Wedding celebrations lasted four days back then. The first day was the procession when I came over on the boat in the afternoon. The next day was spent celebrating with the family. The third day we held festivities with the neighborhood and the last day was with friends and those who came from off the island. I had my hair made up in the *taka shimada* hairstyle of the day and I had to sleep with my head on a brick at night to keep my coiffure from unraveling. I'll show you photos of the wedding a little later.

"After marrying into the family, I became the okami but as well as being the inn's manager, I also cooked meals for the guests. I only retired from cooking five years ago when my second son took over.

"In those days most of our customers came to eat fresh fish. We weren't fishermen ourselves but we'd call up the Fishermen's Union over on the port next to your house, and order fish whenever we needed it and they'd bring it over. Sometimes people would want geisha, so we would call some over from the mainland to come and entertain the guests. But mostly we used *nakaisan* [female staff] from the island. They wore kimonos, and entertained the guests, but for tips. We never paid them. When the guests left, the nakaisan would hang on their arms while walking them to the ferry, and the guests would stick bills inside the front layers of the ladies' kimonos."

Non-acceptance

"The nakaisan were treated as outsiders, all of them, just because they were entertainers. So that was unfortunate.

"When I first came to the inn I was bullied for being the youngest. I also wasn't accepted because I'm an outsider and because I came from a rich family. We call not being accepted into a community *murahachibu*. I'm still not accepted here. That's why even now I don't leave my house very often. You've never seen me at one of those island business meetings, have you? That's because if I attend something like that, there won't be a chair for me. No one will make room for me to sit down. So I just don't go.

"Every morning I put my list of grocery items on the front step and Keiko's husband from the grocery store picks up the list and later delivers the provisions to my house. They send the bill to the Nakan-ishiya, where my daughter-in-law pays it from my pension.

"I have fourteen grandchildren and ten great grandchildren! It's handy having so many family members. When I need to go to the mainland for my check-ups, my daughter or someone else picks me up and takes me to the hospital. They pay for everything. I'm friends with the doctor and all the staff there. They all know me.

"I don't mind sitting here in my house though. I make handicrafts," she says showing me a basket full of *sarubobo*, doll-like amulets she has made from excess kimono material. "I used to make a hundred of these dolls in one day. But I enjoy it. I love sewing and I trained for two years in sewing kimonos when I was young. I made the kimono I'm wearing now. I sometimes alter them a bit, maybe cut the sleeves back or shorten them to just above the knee so I can move easier." She's wearing baggy pants under three layers of kimono, each edge of brocade on top of the next so they fan out into a lovely V-neck. On top of these she wears a white smock so as not to dirty her outfit while cooking or doing chores. "When a kimono gets dirty, I remove the neckpiece, wash it, then sew it back on. I love doing that! I always look forward to it.

"In the summer I often wear Western clothes but I always wear a kimono in the winter because they're warm. Whenever I travel, even abroad, I wear a kimono too. I have drawers and drawers of them upstairs! And I'm healthy. I can still hear fine, I can do my handiwork. I just sit here all day looking out at the sea. I see you walk past my window sometimes."

I tell her that I see her too, sitting inside, when I pass.

"Most of my kimonos are silk. I have *hakama* too," she says, referring to the formal skirted trousers tied at the waist.

She takes off up the steep wooden stairs to the second floor and I trot behind her. She slips into a bedroom where she opens up a kimono chest. Traditional Japanese clothing is not hung on hangers, but is stored by folding the clothes into long flat rectangles, then placing them inside thick Japanese washi paper to protect from moisture. Lastly, these wrapped pieces of clothing are placed in a chest built expressly for kimonos, with stacks of shallow oblong drawers hidden behind two panels that open in the manner of French doors.

"This is the hakama that my husband wore at our wedding. And see these kimonos? I sewed all of them. And look here," she says, herding me into another room of kimono chests. "I have a lot in here too!" she laughs with pleasure. "You know the *uchikake* kimono worn at weddings? I still have mine. The long sleeved *furisode* worn for Coming of Age Day? I have that one too. I have kimonos for all the formal occasions."

She brings out a picture album and flips to a snapshot showing herself and her husband, "Papa," on a stage. They're both dressed in elaborate kimono costumes. "Papa would recite Japanese poems and I would dance to them. It's called Shigin Odori. We were the only ones on the island who knew this dance, because you needed money to learn it. We hired a sensei from the mainland to come out and teach just the two of us."

The photo shows the couple prancing across a red-floored stage, both in white *tabi* split-toed socks and spangled robes of thick gold brocade. On top she wears plain white, with airy sleeves that reach to her wrists until she lifts her arm, when the sleeve trundles down to adorn her movements like the wing of a white crane. The solid black background of the hakama is barely noticeable among the shimmering threads of the pattern: golden aristocrat carriages with silver-leafed chrysanthemums, the red carriage wheels overlaid in more gold crests that prompt the garment to shimmer like sequins. Papa's kimono is pastel turquoise on top, with sleeves that hang down like a sheet of blue sky as he slides across the stage. His hakama is emblazoned with staid shades of caramel-colored chrysanthemum blossoms with equally dazzling threads that sparkle in the camera's flash like morning dew on the brown grasses of autumn. A short halberd is tucked into the pleats of his hakama. The couple both have their left arms extended as they cross the platform, their down-stage hands clutching a folding fan opened to expose the pattern of a white river sweeping through scattered flower blossoms. The costumes alone would have cost a fortune.

"We also danced at the annual Respect for the Aged Day event which is where this one was taken. I was about thirty then. We would dance for people when there was a celebration in the neighborhood.

"Papa died four years ago." She glides her index finger over the glossy plastic film over the scrapbook photo, resting it at the bottom of her husband's hakama as if she's just smoothed the pleats. "Aren't these photos great?" she says, reminiscing. She is sitting Japanese style on the floor with her legs tucked beneath her, neck bent while she looks at the scrapbook resting on her knees. Her hair is tied back in an elegant chignon, the same as in the photo, as if she has never really left the stage.

"Here are the only two photos I have of my wedding," she says, taking from the shelf two mottled cardboard-framed photos, each embossed with a crane and a turtle. "In those days, we didn't have a camera. No one did since they cost a lot of money. These were taken by a professional photographer."

In the first photo, both she and her husband are sitting Japanese style, kneeling with their legs tucked under, perched on cushions on top of a tatami-mat floor. Behind them is the alcove with a traditional ink-brush scroll hanging next to a simple ikebana display of white flowers with a pine bough. The newlyweds face the camera squarely. He has donned a hakama with the family crest on it, and she is clad in a finely detailed kimono with an extra-wide obi sash. She is so small, she gets lost in the folds of the luxurious kimono material that drapes over her hips and legs while she is sitting. She wears a traditional white *tsunokakushi* hat under which is secured a traditional *katsura* hair piece. Her young hands are folded gently over her lap. Both bride and groom have placed collapsed folding fans in front of them on the tatami mat.

In the second photo she is standing in front of the alcove and one can more clearly see the pattern on her wedding kimono: black with swirling leaves caught in a wind, and delicate flowering twigs among clouds. The sleeves dangle so far down, they touch the floor.

She moves on to other photos. "This is me with all the staff and the nakaisan in front of the Nakanishiya inn. All the nakaisan wore kimonos," she says, "even those who served food. We all wore them wherever we went then."

The next photo is of her fiftieth wedding anniversary. "Those are all my grandchildren around us." I recognize five or six of them. "When I die, my daughter will burn these photos and all those silk kimonos! Japanese people just throw these things away. It's such a shame."

This incineration of personal possessions is a long-held custom for islanders, since getting rid of things has always been difficult due to the lack of secondhand shops, recycle shops, garbage services, and more recently, a population to hand things down to. It's so expensive to arrange for a truck to come over on the ferry to take materials away that entire Japanese-style houses are disassembled—guts extracted—and their all-natural materials burned on the beach, beam by beam, memory by precious memory.

Twice a year the local temple holds a Buddhist *goma* fire ceremony, believed to have a spiritual cleansing effect, where people can burn items too sentimental to throw out with the dirty garbage. Photos, letters and talismans will be blessed by a *yamabushi* mountain ascetic priest before they are turned to smoke and journey up to the gods for safekeeping. In the elaborate fire ritual, the yamabushi dons deer skins, blows through conch shells, and releases arrows into the sky from hand bows. As a stack of pine logs are torched, the yamabushi slashes a sword in the air to evoke the deity Fudomyo-o, remover of obstacles and destroyer of evil, and the locals chant the Heart Sutra synchronized to the passing of a large *juzu* prayer-bead rope around the perimeter of the fire. In the finale, possessions are eagerly flung into the flames like ingredients into a soup pot. Only the most precious family items are ever kept back by the heirs, and if the family members have been estranged from the island, perhaps not even those.

When I leave Mama-san's house, she thrusts into my hands a paper bag inside of which are oranges, some of her handmade crafts, and the two black-and-white wedding photos. I politely refuse the photos, however, because she has already told me they are the only copies she has.

The next day, when I return from some business on the mainland, I come home to a large envelope sitting on the step of my *genkan* entrance lobby. I recognize the contents immediately: two mottled cardboard-framed photos.

Mother of Eleven

I WAVE GOOD MORNING to the car-ferry captain sitting at the bridge and proceed up the stairs to the deck for the forty-minute ferry ride to the mainland. Today, like most days, the Seto Inland Sea that surrounds the island appears as placid as a lake. No large waves crash against the island's shores and in the summertime, the wind almost completely ceases. But the tranquil surface belies a relentless undersea current that sallies from east to west, and west to east all day long. This is the effect of the larger oceans—the Pacific Ocean (on the east side) and the Japan Sea (on the west side)—that pour water into the Inland Sea at high tide. The process is reversed, drawing water out of the Inland Sea back into the oceans at low tide. At high tide, these two incoming rushes of water from both ends of the Inland Sea must meet somewhere in the middle. This meeting place is Shiraishi Island, which is why, since ancient times, the island has been referred to by seamen as "the waiting place for winds and tides."

During the Edo period (1603–1868), the shogun required daimyo lords to journey to the capital every other year. Those feudal lords and their entourages who traveled by boat via the Seto Inland Sea route found the median line of this tidal change between east and west to be crucial to successfully time their trips. The daimyo from southern Japan plying the Inland Sea route north to Edo (the old name for Tokyo) would anchor at Shiraishi when the wind died and their boats could no longer move via sail. The tide was even more important than the wind, however, as with a favorable outgoing tide, the current could carry them to their destination, even without wind. If, however, the tide was running toward them, only the strongest wind would be able to overcome the tide's force. Thus, the feudal lord's entire entourage of boats would anchor in Shiraishi harbor to wait—up to six hours—until the next favorable tide change.

But these days, with engine powered boats, ferry captains don't have to worry much about the currents of the Inland Sea. Just like Japan's trains, the ferries are punctual and the Shiraishi car ferry has just belched out three hoarse expirations to indicate it is about to leave port. It's precisely eight o'clock. In the nick of time, Taiko appears on deck. She's short, squat, and slightly out of breath. Seeing her bulgy smiling face gives me the feeling you get when you step inside the carriage of a roller coaster—anticipation of oncoming glee and the urge to raise your arms up over the top of your head for added excitement. Taiko is a real spark plug, an absolute hoot. And she has eleven children.

"Amy-san!" she spews out my name as if she had just spotted a rare white buffalo. She plops down in the seat next to mine. I am so looking forward to this ferry ride now.

I first met Taiko when I was hiking the pilgrimage trail on the island one spring day over twenty years ago. The 6-mile (10-kilometer) route through the mountains skirts by traditional Japanese houses, and at one particular point progresses past a structure with garbage spilling across the trail.

It was here that day, as I tiptoed through the garbage along the path that I heard someone shout my name. "Amy-san! Is that you?"

The fact that anyone was living in that ramshackle building struck me as odd. A scrap of corrugated iron hung down over the doorway like a gaping lower lip, obstructing the wide-open door that was already hanging on for dear life by the threads of its hinges. Blue tarps had been secured with rocks over various sections of the roof to mitigate roof leaks. An outside water tap dripped hopelessly next to an outhouse, its dislodged siding having exposed the wall's thatch of mud and bamboo.

"Amy-san! What are you doing?" she asked, genuinely perplexed as I stumbled past her front door.

I had never talked to this woman who knew my name. I didn't even recognize her. "I'm walking the pilgrimage path," I replied.

She proceeded to advise me on the best way to navigate the garbage jungle and gestured toward a descending zig-zag pathway made of scrap stone. Dead tree branches and leaves crunched under my feet down the lengthy winding stairway that finally emptied me out onto the main road where the pilgrimage path picked up again.

I had seen Taiko several times since that day on the mountain. She is always a lively person to talk to, deftly transferring her enthusiasm to whoever is listening.

She moved out of that house in the forest six months ago and is now enjoying a house that stands at sea level. She had become ill and too weak to be climbing the scrap-mined staircase every time she wanted to come and go from her home. The new rented house, in the neighborhood of Torinokuchi, is much newer than her previous abode and sits alone on the coast looking out toward Kitagi Island. Taiko now rides a motorized four-wheeled vehicle like many of the other aged residents who live far from the port.

Today, she had ridden her electric granny cart straight onto the ferry, parked it, then slowly climbed up the stairs to the second-floor deck in back of the captain's bridge.

We've had many a talk over the years, but I realize just now how little I really know about Taiko.

"Taiko, are you from Shiraishi Island?"

"Oh no, I'm from Oshima on the mainland," she says, pointing to a landmass we can see from the deck of the ferry. "I was born four years after the war ended. You know your next door neighbor Kazu-chan? I'm the same age as her, and Mi-chan too."

This reminds me that I happen to have an old 1955 black-and-white photo of Mi-chan that her husband, the Newspaper Delivery Man, gave me. I take out the photo of the six-year-old standing at the ferry port. It's evident Taiko has never seen this photo before. "Wow!" she marvels. "Mi-chan? Look, she's wearing wooden *geta* sandals!"

It's an interesting combination—a little girl wearing a Western-style dress and traditional Japanese wooden sandals on low stilts. There are other people in the photo too, adult women who are clothed the same, frozen in the early Showa era during the transition stage from Japanese kimonos to the new Western-style clothing that was becoming de rigueur.

The next photo I show her is the old wooden ferry full of tourists. "Wow, wow, wow! How nostalgic!" she cries. "Back in those days, Shiraishi was a really popular place, ne? Then she turns her mouth down and says, "Now hardly anyone comes."

I ask after her children, and we chat about them for a while. I know only a few of her kids, including the youngest who left the island upon graduating high school last year. We leave the Showa era and enter the present Reiwa era, as she starts showing me photos stored on her cellphone. When Taiko talks about her children, rather than using their names, she reverts to the Japanese numbering system for offspring: *chonan* (oldest son) is in Shibukawa; *chojo* (eldest daughter) is in Osaka; *jinan* (second son) is in Kasaoka; *nijo* (second daughter) is in Okayama; and *sanjo* (third daughter) is in Tokyo. The rest are in Okayama.

"This is *chonan*" she says, pointing the screen of her cellphone at me. "He looks like that bald singer, Chiharu Matsuyama," she says, cackling at her own joke. "And this is his wife and my grandchild. People think he's a girl! They have a cute cat too," she says, though the cat is not pictured.

"This is *san-nan's* [third boy's] son," she says, moving on to the next picture. This grandson went on a foreign homestay in fourth grade. "Where did he go?" I ask, naturally curious. But Taiko says she doesn't remember which country it was. Instead, she answers, "In sixth grade, he went to Australia. This July he's going somewhere too." But she can't remember where. "He's not going alone, so it's okay. He's going with his school. He lives in Tokyo. Why does he want to go abroad so often?" she wonders.

"My other grandson in Tokyo is twelve years old and comes to Shiraishi every year. He takes a plane all by himself. He stays at *nijo's* house in Okayama, and she picks him up at the airport. But he doesn't stay on the island. He was afraid of my toilet in the old house because it was a pit-style toilet, and he thought he was going to fall in!"

"Mmm," I say, although I suspect it was the house, not the toilet, that he was afraid of.

"By the way, Eiji-kun just got married and his wife is pregnant!"

says Taiko. The last time I saw Eiji, the fifth son and tenth child, he was still a high school student.

"I've been on Shiraishi fifty years," she says, "ever since I married and came as a bride. You remember my husband, Kaoru, right? He just loved drinking, so what could I do? He drank himself to death. That was eighteen years ago."

"So *sueko* [youngest child] was still in elementary school then?"

"Yes."

We talk about alcohol for a while. "You should drink *shochu*!" she recommends, referring to the local distilled spirit. "Shochu is much healthier than beer!"

I'm doubtful, but don't say anything.

"Do you drink wine?" she asks me. When I answer in the affirmative she says, "It's not very good is it?" and belts out a cackle. "If you're not used to the taste, it's not very good. I can't drink beer or wine, only *nihonshu*," she says, using the term for Japanese sake. "If you refrigerate sake, it's very good. I even drink it cold in the winter."

Her phone jingles and she takes the call. "I'm on the ferry, just arriving at Kasaoka. I have to go to the convenience store to pay a bill. No, it has to be paid at the convenience store. I'll call you when I get back to the island."

"I'm glad I met you today and had a nice long talk," she says as we both shuffle down the stairway and prepare to disembark.

The mechanical ramp is lowered and as the vehicles drive off, Taiko rides past me on her granny-mobile. With a broad smile she puts both hands in the air above her head and flutters her fingers in a happy goodbye wave.

❀ ❀ ❀

Some weeks later, after the day's sun has waned, making the sky glow like a dying ember, I am sitting on the wooden veranda at my friend Tano-san's house in the neighborhood of Torinokuchi. A few other islanders are there too and we're eating oysters and drinking wine. When darkness descends, candles are lit on the open veranda and our glasses of white wine glow like small light globes. A few more torches are lit outside on the pathway while we watch the full moon rise.

I notice some headlights zooming down the hill on the ring road between the house and the water. It's Taiko-san on her electric granny cart. As she cruises down the road next to what used to be a beautiful beach but is now a seawall, we yell out: "Taiko-san, Taiko-san!"

She hears our racket, brings her machine to a halt, and we yell out again, "Taiko-san, Taiko-san, come and join us!" She parks the vehicle on the road and walks up to the house. She is all smiles, as usual, and looks upon us as if she has just discovered a pool of hippos in a bog. "Waaaa, what are you all doing?" she says.

Even in daylight Taiko looks about fifty but in fact is twenty years older. Her face is round, her hair cropped short like a man's, and her skin looks just as smooth in the sunshine as it does in the glow of the candles. Have some fresh oysters! we offer, but she laughs and declines. "I've just had dinner," she says. We offer her a chair to sit on in the garden facing the veranda, and although it's a small canvas camping chair made for fishing, she settles in perfectly comfortably.

Someone says, "Taiko-san, I was trying to remember the names of all your children the other day, but could only come up with ten. Who am I missing? There was the one who was my classmate, then…" and they go through the list of names. "Oh yes, I had him when I was forty-two," she says, ticking them off one by one. "*Sueko* [youngest child] just married last year. She's thirty and my oldest is fifty now."

After they've located the missing name, the conversation turns to Taiko's deceased husband, Kaoru, whom only the Tanos hadn't ever met.

"Oh, he was a wild one," Taiko says. "He was only good at planting seeds!" she says as if she were a farmer's wife. But Kaoru was a carpenter.

"He'd be off the island for days at a time on a job, then come home one night, leave for a week and I'd be pregnant again!" she says laughing. "Yep, planting seeds was the only thing he was good at! He used to have a lot of women on the mainland, too you know. Sometimes he'd bring them to the island. He'd bring them here to the house!"

"Ehhhh? No way!" Her audience tuts at the husband's audacity.

"Then I'd have to feed them dinner," says Taiko.

We're dumbfounded.

"If it got too late," Taiko continues, "and the last ferry had left the island, I'd say very politely, 'So, *o-josama* [lofty girlfriend], will you be staying with us overnight?' And she'd say, 'Oh, no!' surprised at being asked such a question by the wife."

Now we are all laughing in disbelief, not at the veracity of Taiko's story, but at the preposterous days of yore, when women were expected to put up with philandering men.

She continues: "Then I'd turn to my husband and say, 'How about you, Kaoru? Will you be staying here overnight?' If they were both still here in the morning, I'd feed them breakfast. Then he'd disappear for another few days.

"Sometimes he would come back after being gone a week or so, and when doing his laundry, I'd notice he had new, cute underwear. 'Oh, did your girlfriend buy those for you?' I'd say. He'd always get a bit ruffled when I asked anything about his forays.

"I can say all this now only because he's dead. He's probably up there looking down at us laughing. But he's not here, so I can say anything I want now."

Taiko is still smiling, but with melancholy. The only thing I see looking down on us is the full moon.

"Thinking about those times now, they were the best," says Taiko, "because I had all my kids here with me then. Now everyone's gone."

The Cargo Ship Captain

"I'M SIXTY-TWO NOW, born in the Year of the Rooster. My brother and I are boat captains. My father was too. My brother is the first-born, and his name is Ken, and I'm the second born, but my name is Hideichiro, so everyone thinks I'm the first born!" he says, referring to the naming of sons according to the order they are born: -taro, -ichiro (first son); -jiro (second son); -saburo (third son); -shiro (fourth son); -goro (fifth son); -rokuro (sixth son); -shichiro (seventh son); Hachiro (eighth son); Kuro (ninth son); Juro (tenth son); and Juichiro (eleventh son).

"My father was the first born but his name was Kiku-o, using the kanji characters for 'chrysanthemum.' First born sons in those days sometimes had *kiku* in their name.

"Before the war, it was normal to have a lot of children. My father had nine siblings in his family and my mother had six because, you know, 'Be fruitful and multiply!'" he says, quoting the wartime slogan. "In those days, there could be as much as twenty years difference between the oldest and youngest. My father was older than his uncle! There's a lot of that on Shiraishi because people had so many children.

"For a long time I thought my father was the oldest of his siblings but it turns out he had an older sister! I didn't know because she wasn't around when I was a kid.

"Did you know Kaoru?" I ask him. "The guy with eleven kids?"

"Kaoru was a carpenter. He had just nine children for a while but he liked to drink. Once he was drunk he'd say, 'Oh, more kids is fine!' So then they had the tenth child. He kept drinking and then they had the eleventh! Even though Kaoru and Taiko had their children after the war, the war days weren't that far behind. There was no birth control like nowadays and they both came from families with a lot of siblings. Sometimes a family would give their most recent child a name based on a naming superstition. For example, if a couple didn't want any more children, they'd name their child Tome, which comes from the word *tomeru* [to stop], in the hope that no more children would be born. One of my classmates had four daughters. He and his wife didn't want more children unless they could have a boy. So they named the fourth girl Nozomi [wish] and prayed for a boy next. The next child turned out to be a boy!

"I knew some fraternal twins whose parents named them Tome-kichi and Sueko [youngest]. But their parents still had another child after that! By then they had too many children, so they allowed another couple who didn't have any kids to adopt the twins. But even after that, the twins' parents still produced two more children!"

School Days

"What was it like on the island when you were going to school?" I ask Hideichiro. We're sitting on the beach enjoying cans of beer at sunset. Hideichiro, bald as a Buddhist priest and portly as the laughing Buddha, has fond memories of his island childhood.

"People one cycle older than me didn't go to high school. They didn't have the money. [One cycle equals twelve years according to the Chinese zodiac.] So they went straight into work on the boats. Some went to captain's school but on Shiraishi not so many boys did because we learned everything from our fathers and their friends. But going to captain's school was advantageous because they paid for your food and accommodation. So a lot of families on the mainland wanted their sons to go. Even if you never got a job on a boat after graduating, it was good to go to captain's school for those reasons.

"Captains made good money too. When I was in school, not many kids had softball gloves because they were expensive. But my father bought me one. Kids didn't have bats either. Heck, we didn't even have bicycles then! My grandfather's younger brother ran Harakuni, a dry goods store on the island. They used bicycles to deliver goods to houses, but most people couldn't afford one. When I was born it was Showa 32 [1957], so twelve years after the war, but still, living was tough here. It wasn't for another decade that people on Shiraishi started to have more money.

"I was a bit of a troublemaker when I was young. I'd see someone on the street and say, 'Hey, why you looking at me?' I was arrogant. Now that I think about it, I can't believe I acted that way. I had a lot of fun though. I think everyone should just have fun.

"I've known my wife since we were kids. We were classmates. Eight of my classmates are still on the island. We don't get together that much like some of the other classes. Tomekichi's classmates were all born in the year of the dragon and the year of the snake, which is said to be a good combination. So they always have classmate get-togethers at their houses. My class is made up of the year of the monkey and chicken. Not such a good combination."

Ceremonies and Festivals

"One thing I remember well happened when I was in sixth grade. That's when the Bussharito [Thai-style stupa] was built. You know the Bussharito holds some of the bones of the Buddha. There aren't many of those around Japan, so it was a big deal when they held the opening ceremony. Everyone on the island went. All us students lined up to greet the visiting Thai Buddhist priests. We were given little paper Japanese and Thai flags to wave and I remember the Thai priests wore straw sandals.

"There used to be food stalls set up at all the festivals because we had a much bigger population back then. Like at the Fall Festival, people would line up in front of the *torii* gate of the Shinto shrine to wait their turn to carry their neighborhoods *mikoshi* portable shrine down from the main shrine. There were even fights back in those days. Everyone would drink too much, and, you know, one neighborhood would be carrying their mikoshi up the narrow street, and another neighborhood would be carrying theirs down. No one wanted to have to back up to let the others by, so they'd fight!

"Nowadays people don't put so much effort into the festivals. It used to be that people worked really hard for their community and for their families. When Yosaburo was the head of the Shiraishi Bon Dance, his younger brother had already been working long days at the JA [Japan Agricultural co-operative] office making deliveries and such. He hardly ever took a day off. By the time the summer came around, he was really overdoing it preparing for that year's dance. On the night of the dance, he had a stroke and died. Think about it, he was preparing for the Shiraishi dance, a dance that honors the dead.

"Kazu-chan's husband," he says, referring to my next-door neighbor, "also worked long hours in the heat all summer long and he also had a stroke.

"There used to be a *toban* rotation system where each year a different neighborhood hosted the festival, but that stopped several years ago too. Some neighborhoods don't even carry their mikoshi at the Fall Festival anymore because there aren't enough people to muscle it up that long hill to the Shinto shrine. And some people are too old to come out and party like that. Then there's the exclusion rule for those who have had a family member pass away in the past year. Out of the respect for the deceased, they have to wait out one year of all island celebrations. With so many elderly on the island, almost everyone has a relative who's died recently! And there are so few kids around. Without children there's no meaning anymore. You're just going through the motions. What's the point if you can't pass down the traditions to someone?"

The Kaisei Maru Cargo Ship

"My brother and I bought our cargo ship in November of 1996. We used that boat to transport spools of steel cables up and down the Inland Sea. Do you remember the *mochinage* rice-cake-throwing ceremony we held to inaugurate the boat?"

I do. It was an island-wide event where locals tried their hand at catching pouches of sweets tossed into the crowd from the bow of the new ship. Some rice cakes were white, some were pink, others had 500-yen coins hidden inside them. It's said to be good luck to eat rice cakes from a boat's mochinage ceremony. It's also believed to be fortunate if a pregnant woman attends, and if so, she should be invited on board the ship to throw the rice cakes.

"It seems so long ago now," says Hideichiro. "That was probably the last mochinage ceremony ever held for a boat on Shiraishi Island. I doubt there will ever be another."

"Do you miss being on the boat?" I ask, referring to his recent retirement.

"Sometimes. But other times it's a relief. I don't have to worry about the weather anymore, like storms and typhoons, or about docking such a large ship. We've had a couple accidents, you know. One time in a storm, a cargo ship moored next to ours drifted into our boat and smashed it up. Another incident occurred with one of those cranes that lifts metal using a big magnet. Well, the crane dropped a metal spool onto our boat before it had reached its target.

"The steel factories used to send lots of scrap metal to China. Those boats often have fires on board because the materials scrape against each other and the friction produces sparks which sometimes set the oil on fire. Whenever I'd see those boats we'd tie up way on the other side of the pier.

"It would be nice if there were no accidents, but no matter how much you take care, they happen."

Hideichiro's Accident

"There are many times in my life when I thought I would die. I've had a few accidents and everyone always says I won't survive the next one. I realize now that I'm tempting fate because this last time I was very close to ending up in a grave on Tomiyama Hill.

It happened at seven thirty in the evening. I crashed my scooter, banging my head on the ground and also twisting my neck. I wasn't wearing a helmet either. I didn't feel any pain though because I was drunk! A fishermen from my neighborhood was going home on his scooter when he saw me lying on the road. I'd been lying there bleeding for three hours before he came along.

"I'm a big guy so it took five men from our fire department to haul me to the port. The Kairyu Maru [emergency charter boat] took me to the mainland and they said I snored all the way there! My daughter was at the port waiting with the ambulance and she said she could see part of my skull sticking out of my head. At any rate, the hospital told my family they didn't think I'd be able to walk again. So they came back to the island and cleaned out the house since I wouldn't be coming back. My older brother figured I wouldn't be able to work again so he sold the cargo ship to a company in Singapore. I was in the hospital two and a half months and did lots of rehabilitation. I can walk now but I can't work anymore. I guess it wasn't quite time for me to move to Tomiyama Hill," he says with a chuckle.

And that is how one accident brought the abrupt end to a seafaring lineage.

"When I think back on my accident, I think it was a good thing. My brother is trimming bonsai trees and enjoying his Harley Davidson now. He has a Harley group that goes everywhere, like to Hokkaido and New Zealand. I can move okay now but I can't walk too far. I go places in my car or play mahjong. But when I'm out I don't drink if I have to drive home. So I just drink at my house. Or like today, I'm having a drink on the beach because I can walk home from here."

The Okami

ONE OF SHIRAISHI'S RITES of summer is the festival to pay homage to Benzaiten, goddess of the sea, who lives on a tiny island off the beach. This small celebration is maintained by Mama-san's second son and takes place at the lowest tide of the season. At any other time, the sandbar that leads to the island is submerged, so the goddess can only be visited by boat. But on the appointed day, the water will ebb just enough to be able to walk across the temporarily exposed sandbar to an outcropping of sea-sculpted rocks and crooked pine trees. From there, a set of stairs passes under a *torii* gate dividing the sacred world of the goddess from the mundane world of mortals. At the top of the steps is a red-painted shrine with the cyan curl of a wave brushed onto its side. During this once-a-year ceremony, a priest unlocks the doors of the small vestibule, and from the darkness of an entire year, the deity emerges. Among offerings of Japanese sake, sacred *sakaki* branches, a ripe pink peach, and a freshly sacrificed red snapper, the locals perform austerities to the goddess of the sea.

After the festival, I stop at the beachside Nakanishiya Inn that the Mama-san used to lord over. Her daughter-in-law, Fumi, has just come back from the festival and will soon rush off to another appointment, but says she can spare for few minutes for me. Fumi married Mama-san's first son, who inherited the inn. It was natural that Fumi would eventually take over as the *okami* upon Mama-san's retirement. The inn is currently run by this husband and wife team the way most businesses are on Shiraishi Island.

"I'm originally from Kitagi Island," she tells me. "My family was in the stone business. When I married into this family, I started working here right away.

"We have twenty rooms and eighty futons at this inn. We can hold eighty people but we're never completely full unless we have a group.

In the old days you could put four people in a room, but nowadays people want more space, so unless it's a group, you can't do that.

"Even though we never had as many people in the wintertime compared to summer, we still held company banquets, farewell parties, welcome fetes, and such." Banquets for fifty to a hundred people required special food and decorations appropriate to the occasion. "For celebrations such as weddings, we used the symbolic *shochikubai* (pine, bamboo and plum), or the crane and turtle as a motif. For funerals, on the other hand, the lotus flower was more appropriate as it is the symbol of enlightenment."

The Nakanishiya had a solid business serving meals for the Buddhist memorial ceremonies that are held at set intervals after a person's death, always on odd-numbered years. The first ceremony is held on the first anniversary of one's passing, then on the seventh anniversary, the thirteenth, seventeenth, and twenty-third. The final ceremony commemorates the fiftieth anniversary. All the relatives would come to the island for these tributes and the inns provided meals as well as rooms for those coming from out of town. But as the population has declined, so have the attendees of the memorial services.

"Now we don't have as many customers coming to enjoy the sea in the summertime because these days people prefer to go to air-conditioned shopping malls or Tokyo Disneyland, or even Europe. Local places like Shiraishi are no longer popular. But you know, there are two kinds of guests: those who like to have others around them and those who prefer to be alone. Some like to come here because they can have the beach to themselves. Of course I enjoy it when a lot of people come, but I like it when it's quiet too. And nowadays, people are interested in finding secret places that are off the beaten track.

"When you compare now to the old days though, it's a bit of a shame. When I sit here and look over to the city of Fukuyama on the mainland, I feel as if I'm in that anime *Nokosarejima* ['Lost Island']."

I walk home from the Nakanishiya via Tomiyama Hill. At the foot of the incline I pass a house that was abandoned years ago. Japanese people call such rundown buildings ghost houses because they've been there so long that by now ghosts must inhabit them. While most people, like the Stone Bridge Lady, still look after their empty houses, other dwellings fall into neglect as their owners have either passed on or their relatives have moved far away and don't have the time or inclination to come back to perform the upkeep. Luckily, most traditional Japanese houses are made of natural materials: wooden beams; bamboo-thatched walls stuffed with mud; paper doors; and tatami-mat floors. This house on the way up Tomiyama Hill looks as forlorn as a pine tree suffering a slow death of decay. Engulfed in a carpet of weeds, it has been left to rot in nature's embrace.

I continue up the cemetery road and am soon at the top. With only a vague recollection of where I had stood on the forty-ninth day after Eiko's death eighteen years ago, I head up the main path off to the left. About half-way up, I start scanning the head stones. Since most islanders share the same surnames, it won't be easy to find her grave. After twenty minutes, I have seen many Nakagawas but no headstone with Eiko's name. Undeterred, I stray a bit further, moving closer to where the tablets plummeted down the slope in the deluge of the last typhoon. It is only then that I notice a lonely little pillar sitting a perilous few feet from the new drop-off. The head stone is bare of flowers or greenery. While other family tombs have several generations of members' names chiseled on their *kaimyoban* nameplate, this one does not. In fact, the gravestone looks fairly new. On the back, it is written that it was constructed in 2003, the year Eiko died.

Engraved on this pillar are three names: Eiko Nakagawa, died April 12, 2003 at eighty-four years old. Shoichi Nakagawa, died May 27, 1945 at twenty-seven years old. Several things surprise me. First, twenty-six seems rather old to be drafted into war. Second, it seems a travesty that he died so close to the end of the war, during the time of the Battle of Okinawa. But the third name is truly revelatory: Emiko Nakagawa, died April 24, 1947, at three years old.

The Ferry Captains Who Moonlight As Priests

I HAVE BEEN INVITED to attend the Opening of the Sea, a Shinto ceremony, after which the Tenrikyo Priest and his son have promised me an interview. A small gathering of ten people who make their living from businesses on the beach are sitting under a white tent on this July morning that marks the official beginning of beach season on the island. The summer has already started, but the beach doesn't officially open until reverence is paid to the gods. No problem, though—a father and son have arrived to do exactly that.

These two practitioners of the Tenrikyo religion have constructed a makeshift altar on the beach. This stand-alone structure is set off by young, thin bamboo stalks set into the sand in four corners to make a quadrangle. These stalks, still adorned with their fine slim leaves, are joined by a rope festooned with white purification papers that have been twisted into the rope fibers, Shinto-style. Inside this corded sanctuary, a table has been covered with plain white cloth atop which two shelves, an upper and a lower, hold offerings of sake and rice. A freshly caught red snapper is laid out, body still wet, scales sparkling in the sun. A white string has been strung around the tail, passed under the base of the fin and threaded through the snapper's small pearly mouth, with the string ultimately secured to the animal's head via the first spike in its dorsal fringe. The contraption, when pulled taut, coaxes the creature's body into an arabesque with head and tail pointing up toward the gods. The altar glows white against the background of a cobalt blue sky and the indigo hills of the mainland across the sea.

The chanting starts and the Ferry Captain, doubling as Tenrikyo priest, asks the *kami* (divine spirits) to protect Shiraishi Island, its beaches and surroundings. The beach neighborhood, called Nishinoura (lit., west side), is referred to often, and reverence is paid and vows are made to the spirits of the sea.

The priest and his son wear jet-black robes with lengthy sleeves that flutter in the sea breeze. The collar and front V-neck are inlaid with cream colored embroidery that spirals down the fabric, softening an otherwise mournful-looking robe. The matching black hats are of the religious *eboshi* style, tall with a rounded top and a single black tail that hangs past the nape of the neck and down the back. The father's gray hair peeks out the sides, his weatherbeaten face reflecting a life spent on these sun-kissed shores. The son, handsome and slender, plays assistant preparing the sacred *sakaki* branches for the ceremony participants.

Next, each person in attendance, as a representative of their business and their sincere gratitude to the kami, picks up a revered branch and walks to the front of the altar. They each bow to the altar, clap four times, then bow again, before placing the stalk in front of the offerings of fish, sake and rice. With this placement, the participant claps four times again, bows one last time, and returns to their seat.

In the distance, I hear the two long toots as a ferry comes into the port. It must be 10:20.

The Tenrikyo priest closes the ceremony by beseeching the kami to protect our beach, our island and to grant us a safe swimming season. The sake bottles are opened and they make a toast to the kami. People laugh and smack their lips in tribute to how good it is to start drinking so early in the day. The ceremony is over but people linger to talk, make predictions about the upcoming summer beach trade and refill their cups with the free sake.

Meanwhile the Tenrikyo Priest and his son pack up their wares and climb into their van to return to the temple where they live. I am along for the ride because the priest has agreed to tell me the story of Tenrikyo on Shiraishi Island.

At the Temple

The Tenrikyo priest's wife welcomes us into the temple. While she and I chat in the kitchen, the priest leaves to change into something less formal, and a few minutes later reappears barefoot with a T-shirt tucked into comfortable cotton pants with an elastic waistband.

"When I was growing up, it was only about ten years after the end of World War II so our family didn't have much, not even enough to eat sometimes. At least the war dead got some kind of compensation; not us though—we didn't even have that! There was a bread shop just over there—the one that belonged to Panken's parents. The aroma of fresh baked bread would waft across here at night when they were making bread. We would lie in our futons and be so hungry. That bread smelled like heaven. It was absolute torture.

"We lived up on the Narazu mountain behind here. That was where the temple was at that time. There were just two houses up there and we lived in the one next to Taiko-san and Kaoru."

"Is Taiko a follower of Tenrikyo?"

"Her husband's parents were the founding fathers of the Tenrikyo sect here. But Taiko and Kaoru had to quit for a while because they were to busy with all those children to care for.

"Living up there wasn't easy. In those days, we had to fetch water from the spring at the bottom of the hill and carry it up all those steps because there was no well!"

That zig-zag pathway made of scrap stone?

"It was tough, I tell you. Then, in the back of the temple were the gardens and after harvesting the potatoes we had to carry them out on our backs. They were so heavy! I don't like to remember those times, or even talk about them. But the Tenrikyo temple was good to us. We could eat there and they helped us get by. That's why I'm dedicated to Tenrikyo now, because I have to give something back. We built the new temple here eight years ago because the other temple up on the mountain was falling apart."

While the island doesn't have many Tenrikyo followers these days, the temple is serving a larger purpose by continuing observances such as the Opening of the Sea, which most people feel can be conducted by any old priest, as long as he can communicate with the kami. In fact, before the Tenrikyo priest administered this Shinto ceremony, it was conducted by the local Buddhist priest.

But the Tenrikyo Priest's day job is at the wheel of a boat.

Boat Captains

"Our neighborhood, Torinokuchi, is mostly boat captains. There's Hideichiro and Ken from the Kaisei Maru, and the captain from the Bizen Maru. Across the street from us is another captain. The guy next door had an accident and has retired now, but he was on a boat. The guy who was at the helm of the emergency boat, the Kairyu Maru lives in this neighborhood too. There used to be others as well.

"I've been piloting the car ferry about thirty-three years now. I captained the old wooden one for three years before it was changed over to a more modern steel version. The wooden rig was bigger, and we could fit fourteen or fifteen cars and trucks on that ferry. Now the ferry is smaller.

"When the weather gets rough, we have to stop the ferry service. The rule is that if the wind speed is over 15 meters [50 feet] per second, we can't leave the port, but if we're not comfortable with the weather, we can decline to leave port too. But honestly, I think the weather was worse back in the old days. The boats are better now too so they handle rougher seas. I work in the office most of the time now, and my son does the rest of it.

"What's the biggest change on the island since I was a kid? Well, we had a larger population in the old days and we used to lose about twenty-four people a year. But we always knew when someone passed away, and we went to all the funerals. But these days since so many people moved to Kasaoka on the mainland, they pass away there, and have their funerals over there, so we don't even know they died! And we don't notice either how much the population has decreased here. You just look around every now and then and think, wow, not many people left!

"When I wake up in the morning and open my eyes, I'm just

happy to be alive. I think it's important that we always thank the gods that we live a good, happy life."

The Tenrikyo Priest's wife has been uncannily silent. When I look her way, she gives me a shy smile. I was so engrossed in her husband's talk I hadn't noticed she put cold barley tea and two individually wrapped rice crackers in front of me.

The Son

"Can you tell me about Tenrikyo?" I ask.

"It's very difficult," he says.

"Just the basics. Act like you're explaining Tenrikyo to a three-year-old," I tell him.

"Okay," he agrees. "To put it simply, the Tenrikyo doctrine says that the gods were created to show that humans could live a happy life. This is our philosophy. The religion was developed at the end of the Edo period, between 1853 and 1867. It used to be related to Shinto but now it is completely separate."

"What are the hand movements that I see the women perform?"

"Oh, the hand dance? Through the Tenrikyo hand movements we can pray for things like world peace, a joyful life, or even to help those in trouble.

"Now I'll tell you the story of how Tenrikyo came to the island. One day one of the island boys, when he was four years old, was playing on two boats that were tied together. He caught his right arm between the boats and ended up losing the use of his hand. In those days, things weren't so good for disabled people, so he went to work in Narazu, up on the mountain where he could work on his own. While he was living there, a proselytizer came by and told him about the Tenrikyo religion. He learned how he could heal his hand by following Tenrikyo. He thought this was something special and wanted to spread it around Shiraishi. In those days there were many converts on the island, and in Showa 52 (1977), five years before I was born, the first worship house was built. I'm the fourth generation Tenrikyo practitioner on Shiraishi."

"How many followers are there on the island now?" I ask.

"Now, not so many. My mother, my father, my grandmother, Taiko-san and me, so five people."

"Wow, and you just built that gorgeous new temple?"

"Yes, the Tenrikyo headquarters helped with that. I was a Tenrikyo missionary in Osaka for a year and I did a lot of other jobs on the mainland for a while. I came home because my father said they needed crew on the ferry. I was thirty-one then. I'm forty now. None of my classmates are still on the island. They've all moved away."

"With the decreasing population, what do you think will happen to the ferry service in the future?"

"As long as people are living here, there has to be a transportation service, so I think there will always be a ferry, and if the management company gets to the point it can't survive anymore, the city will probably help continue it. Right now there are four full-time people working on the boat who rotate shifts."

"Are you glad you came back to live on the island?"

"I think so. It's a bit inconvenient but once you get used to it, it's fine. But until you get to that point, it's tough. It's not as hard for me because I'm from here, but others who might want to move here would find it difficult. Soon there will be no school and the doctor only comes twice a week. And people who come from outside need a long time for island people to get to know them and accept them. As people get older, they become more inflexible in their views. And they don't understand change. So it would be better if we had more young people on the island. As the population gets older and smaller, they'll have to let more people in eventually."

I finish my cup of barley tea and the son's mother beams a shy smile to me from the other side of the table. Before I leave, she insists I take the uneaten rice crackers home with me and stuffs them into my pocket.

The Runaway

WITH THE OPENING OF THE SEA CEREMONY completed, the beach season stretches out lazily in front of us. Schoolchildren are on vacation and families from the mainland are starting to make day-trips to the island. The inns and beach shacks are just beginning to hum with their summer trade.

The Insect Festival has also just taken place, in which all undesirable pests were serenaded by villagers who, while shouldering a miniature wooden boat, paraded down the road from temple to sea, chanting to the rhythmic striking of a *taiko* drum:

> For a good harvest, insects go away!
> For a good harvest, insects go away!
> Root eaters, leaf eaters, we send you all away!"

The chagrined pests, reconciled to their fate, board the palanquin, and when they arrive at the beach, the vessel is launched into the waves and gently pushed from the shore as the Buddhist Priest offers prayers and bellows through his bullhorn infinite farewells.

❉ ❉ ❉

On a sweltering day, I am sitting inside the former Amasaka Inn while the proprietress chips at a large block of ice with a pick. She plunks a lengthy shard into a glass with a clink and fills it with oolong tea for me. "Is that the same block you use to make shaved ice?" I ask her, referring to the popular Japanese summertime beach treat.

"Yes. There's a place in Kasaoka that makes these large ice blocks. They put about ten blocks into a thick paper bag and send them over to me on the ferry."

I glance doubtfully at her aging shaved-ice machine that looks ready, at any moment, to give up its summer part-time job. She drags her slippered feet, swish-swish, back over to the table and sits down in a cracked plastic seat.

Mimiko was born in Showa 19 (1944), a time when nearly two thousand people made their living on Shiraishi Island. Traditional Japanese-style inns like Amasaka provided amusement for mainland families who took the ferry out to Shiraishi on weekends to eat fresh fish, play on the island's beaches and dig for *asari* clams. Amasaka overlooks the beach and the second floor tatami-matted guest rooms faced the sea. The ground floor was reserved for cooking and serving the breakfast and dinners included in the guests' board. Since most of their seaside home was devoted to the business, the family lived in two bedrooms off the corridor adjacent to the kitchen.

Mimiko lives in Tokyo but comes back every summer to run Amasaka, which has been reduced to a beach shack selling draft beer, snacks and shaved ice.

"I'll never forget when Mama-san came to the island," she says. "It was before the concrete road was laid along the shore. Back then, our house and all the other beach businesses butted right up to the beach, and the guests unloaded themselves from the wooden ferry and walked through the interior to get to the beach. I remember once when I was about nine years old, standing in front of our house, looking out at the water. Coming out from between two houses, I saw this woman, elegant in a red *uchikake* wedding kimono and high clogs. She had a broad, white-powdered face and she wore a white *tsunokakushi* wedding hat. Her lips were tinted crimson. As soon as she stepped out onto the beach, everyone turned their heads. 'Well, look at Kenjiro's new wife!' they all said. They couldn't hide their surprise. Everyone agreed she was the most beautiful woman on the island."

In those days the bride always moved to the groom's home, and if he was the first-born son, she would live together with him and her new in-laws. This new flow of wives from outside the island provided much excitement for the residents, who scrutinized each woman upon arrival.

But fifty-seven years ago, when Mimiko was in her last year of high school she had been hoping for a future containing more than salty seas, mainland guests and arranged marriage. So she fled to a place so distant, you couldn't even see it on a clear day from the shores of Shiraishi Island.

"I became a *ronin* [school drop-out] and waited out my last year of school. I finished high school in Tokyo. After graduation, I stayed in the capital and worked as an office lady for six years. I still drop by that office every now and then to say hello. During that time I met my husband, Hirotoshi, who was working for a bank, and we started meeting for dinner after work. He begged me to marry him but I didn't want to marry yet, so I said no. But we continued dating."

She stops for a moment, cocks her head and says, "You've read *The Tale of Genji*, right?"

I nod.

"My husband was like the hero, Shining Genji—all the girls wanted him! After he had his stroke, and six months before he died, I found love letters in his paperback books," she says. 'What are these?' I asked, infuriated. He said, 'Oh, those were from before we were married, when I was working at the bank.'"

At Japanese companies, especially in those days, the office ladies all hoped they would meet someone at the company to marry. Then, they'd quit their jobs.

"Hirotoshi had a locker on the second floor where he'd change out of his bank uniform at the end of the day. The girls would leave love letters in the pockets of his suits! Things like 'I want to marry you' or 'I'm sad when I'm far away from you.' So I asked him 'Did you date them?' He said, 'No, I couldn't date women at work.' It's true that companies had a strict rule not to date cohorts."

So if you did, and many of course couldn't resist, the relationship had to remain top secret, including pretending you didn't like someone just so your colleagues wouldn't suspect you did.

"I'm so glad I didn't know about those letters then," she says. "Because if I had, I never would have married him! I'd have thought he might cheat on me."

"Hirotoshi's dream had been to go to Keio University and study economics. So when he took the Keio entrance exam and didn't pass, he was shocked. He was very smart, and he just couldn't believe he didn't make the grade. But at that time, if you slipped the school some money before the exam, they would give you priority at private universities. Hirotoshi's mother was willing to borrow the money to get him in through the back door, but he didn't want her to do that so instead, he went to work at the bank."

Eventually Hirotoshi prevailed upon Mimiko to tie the knot and they enjoyed forty-five years together.

"When I was twenty-seven, my father died. In those days, my family had a telephone because they ran the inn, but still, you had to dial the Central Post and Telecommunications on the island to put a call through. One day my father called the post office and said he wasn't feeling well. The staff there said, 'Amasaka called and we can't understand a word he's saying. Something must be wrong.' So they sent someone around to check on him. When they came into the house, he was sitting at the table dead, the phone still in his hand.

"So, from then on, I returned yearly to help my mother run this place in the summertime. I had my job in Tokyo, so I couldn't stay the full summer though."

The now dilapidated former inn has been painted over so many times, all the layers of color are peeling.

"My mother also sold fish. She was very good at skinning eels. She'd pound a stake in its head to keep it from escaping, then make a beautiful, clean cut down the entire length of the body in one go. She was really skilled. I can't do that at all!

"Eventually, my mother closed the inn and managed only the beach shack."

Everyone still called her mother Amasaka. When the ninety-seven-year-old died, she left her daughter the remnants of the inn and a fourteen-year-old cat named Mimi. That's when Mitsuko changed her name to Mimiko, in tribute to the cat.

I met Mimiko after her feline name change. Ever since I've known her, she has brought two cats with her from Tokyo on the summer trip home: Mimi, and a tomcat named Eita. When September comes around, she closes up the beach shack, puts them back into their pet carriers, boards the ferry to the mainland then takes them back to Tokyo on the bullet train.

"This summer business nets me just enough to pay the annual land tax on the building and the utility charges." The abandoned second floor is appropriated every August during the Bon festival by the Shiraishi Bon Dance troupe to change into their traditional costumes before performing on the beach.

The first floor of the accommodation looks as if someone had shut up shop fifty years ago, tossed the key and walked away. If a guest from back in the day came to visit—and they occasionally do—they'd find it just as they remembered from childhood. The hand-cranked shaved ice machine sits irreverently in the corner. On the walls, inked paper portraits of sumo wrestlers of yore curl at the corners. Aging display fridges that refuse to chill, now feature stuffed animals of equal vintage peering out. The only thing new is another layer of the yellowish, salt-encrusted patina of fifty years of sea breezes.

Among this stubborn array of artifacts rooted in laziness and nostalgia, Mimiko orchestrates a bustling, yet punctuated, summertime trade. These days the tables serve teenyboppers who hunker down over piping-hot curry rice received through the kitchen window. Junior high school students pay one hundred yen for boiling water to pour into their cups of store-bought instant noodles. Beach-goers plop two one-hundred-yen coins into the "honor box" while shimmying in and out of rickety shower stalls.

Suddenly we're interrupted by the five o'clock bell, which also means the last ferry to "the land," as the locals call it, will leave in forty minutes. Mimiko's showers start humming and the aging floorboards of the shower stalls creak under sandy feet. The proprietress starts rapping on the shower stall doors encouraging the young teenage beach bums to "hurry up" so the next person gets a chance to shower.

In another hour, the tourists will be gone, and the sun will have started to pale. The locals will drift out of their homes on the faint wafts of coolness to come to Amasaka to re-enact the good ole days.

Soon Mimiko, herself no spring chicken, will be serving draft beers and curry-rice leftovers to her former classmates, neighbors and ex-lovers who have come out for the evening—all brought together through Mimiko's enduring friendship. Even the bewhiskered gentleman and his fishing dog will stop by for a spell to see Mimiko, just to catch up and check up on each other.

But before all this happens, I thank Mimiko for the tea and take my leave. She knows I will come back soon. I always do.

When I stop into Mimiko's beach shack a couple days later, Ma-kun, who goes out fishing every morning with Mr. Kawata, is sitting at the table with her. He visits Mimiko every day when she's back for the summer. She gives him iced coffee and snacks in return for his help with simple tasks, such as fetching the heavy ice blocks from the freezer to make shaved ice when she gets busy. I sit down in the empty chair at the table. Mimiko nudges two *mochi* rice cakes in my direction. "This one has sweet bean paste inside, the other has none," she says. I choose the *kusamochi*, the green one with the bean paste. "By the way, I just heard Kio-chan passed away in the spring," she says.

"Really?" I had no idea. Kiofumi Watanabe was well-known for his love of the island festivals and for his predilection for wearing crazy outfits and drinking white wine on such occasions. I immediately think to express my condolences to his family, but I don't think I know any of them. "Does Kio-chan have brothers and sisters on the island?"

"I don't know if he does anymore, but he used to have several siblings. You know, Shiraishi people all have the same names: Harada, Amano, Nishihara, Kawata, Yamakawa, Nakagawa. So when you hear names like Watanabe or Umakoshi you know they're outsiders. So Kio-chan may not have many relatives here."

Funerals

"So you want to know about funeral customs? Well, when my father died, we just assembled family and friends to shovel a grave. When digging a grave, it's best if you get at least one stone quarrier because they're good at digging holes. The grave was always dug the night before the funeral.

"We put a lot of effort into the funeral cortege. Everyone had a role, but we had to decide who would do what, according to degree of kinship. Naturally, my mother was the closest with my father, so she carried the *ihai* [spirit tablet]. Next in importance in the procession were my younger brother and me. After that ranked relatives, then friends of my father. It was supposed to be that the people who were closest to the deceased would carry the casket, but people argued about who was a better friend, so that order took a long time to decide.

"The body was carried in a round *kanoke* [wooden barrel casket] hung from two big pieces of wood that the men hoisted onto their shoulders. You know the place in the graveyard with the six Jizo statues who guard the six realms of the Buddhist afterlife? There's a small hut near there that the priest used for funerals. We set the casket down there, and the Buddhist Priest chanted the sutras in front of that building from a big red chair, called a *kyokuroku*. The priest stopped using that hut when cremations became the norm.

"But when my father was buried, funerals spanned an entire week. Morning and night, we went to the grave to perform Buddhist devotions. We prepared special food: miso soup, tofu, all extravagant foods at the time. When a grandparent died, it was called "New Year for the grandkids" because the grandchildren were happy to have a rare chance to eat nice food! Nowadays we just have a small ceremony and the funeral is finished.

"Once I gave my father a very nice set of nail clippers made in Germany. He really loved those nail clippers, so when he died, we put them in the casket with him. I imagine they're a bit rusty now. Sometimes we'd wonder how our father was doing and thought maybe we should dig him up and see. You know, because we have a burial spot inside the crypt of the Bussharito that we purchased when the stupa was built. We thought of moving him there. Then we could find out if the nail clippers were still there too.

"You know, my father had a role in the Grand Ceremony for the opening of the Bussharito. It was a big deal on Shiraishi at that time. All up and down the road between the port and the temple, lanterns were strung up. High priests from Mount Koya and Thailand came. My father wore a formal kimono with the family crest on it and was honored with the job of meeting the visiting monks from Thailand at the port.

"So we really considered exhuming my father and moving him up to the Bussharito. But it would have been a big project to move him. We'd have had to call in a stonemason and all. In the end, we decided it wasn't worth it.

"When my husband was alive, I told him that if I died first, I wanted to be buried here on Shiraishi Island. But my husband died before me, and he was interred next to his parents in Tokyo. Now I'm reconsidering where I want to be laid to rest. Since we never had children, there's no one here to look after the family tombs. I don't even have any close relatives left on the island. So I'll become *muenbotoke* [an abandoned spirit, with no one to look after the grave].

"Where I live in Tokyo, they have a caretaker at the temple. Once you enter the Buddhist gate, if you turn to the right, you'll find the temple office where you can buy flowers and incense to take to the family plot. But in the countryside there's no system like that.

"So I'm thinking of telling the priest here that I don't need the island graves anymore, nor the one at the Bussharito. He'll come and take out the *tamashi* [spirits] of my ancestors then discard the stones.

"I do what I can for my family's graves but some day I won't be here either."

She ends her soliloquy on this somber note, but then asks,

"Would you like to see my family's plot?"

Of course I would.

Mimiko tells Ma-kun to look after the shop while she's gone. "If anyone comes, tell them I'll be right back."

Mimiko's beach shack is next to the path called Bonsan Michi, which means "Priest's Way" since it is the well-trodden route of the Buddhist Priest. The word for priest in Japanese is *bo-san* but in local Shiraishi fashion, the pronunciation has been changed to suit the tongues of the locals. The road that winds around from the port to the temple is the Daishi Michi, named after the Buddhist saint Kobo Daishi who is said to have visited the island in the ninth century. This name too has been altered to suit the locals, who have always called it Taishi Michi.

It takes only five minutes to get to the graves via the Bonsan Michi. As we head up Tomiyama Hill, we pass that abandoned ghost house I'd noticed earlier.

"The people who lived there worked in the stone business," Mimiko informs me. "But they got into debt. So they borrowed money from others on the island to get by. At first, they slowly paid everyone back, but then things got really bad and they couldn't repay the loans. It's a small island, so it must have been tough having to see people every day that you owed money to, and hoping they wouldn't ask you about it. Especially when you know you can't pay it back. So they decided to escape the island one night. They just left the house, put a padlock on the stone-factory doors, and never came back. They're living somewhere on the mainland now, in Okayama City some people say. The son is said to be very good at spending money. They probably declared bankruptcy so that legally they wouldn't have to pay anyone back. But once you've gone bankrupt, you can't vote or travel overseas for a long time."

She's leading me down a long row of gravestones until we finally come to the end, where she starts introducing me to the monoliths. "This is my grandmother, grandfather and father. They died before the crematorium was built in Kasaoka, so they were all buried. In those days, there were two methods of burying people: either in the sitting position, in which case they were put into a round kanoke, or lying down in a long wooden box. My father was a tall man, more like a foreigner. We ordered an extra large kanoke for him. He was buried wearing a kimono, sitting down.

"This is my grandparents' tomb, constructed for the fifty-year anniversary of their passing," she says, referring to a large hat-topped pillar. It's called a *gorinto* (a pagoda-like gravestone representing the elements earth, water, fire, wind and space) and is the largest of all the graves. "This here is my mother's grave. It's only been seven years since she passed away, so it's still smaller than the gorinto. My mother used to study *goeika* sutra songs at the temple, so it's written here on the side of her tombstone: 'She reached level 2 and can teach goeika.' Recently we had the fiftieth anniversary of my father's death," she says, gesturing to the new flowers and other decorations surrounding his grave. She gestures to a statue of a robed Jizo, the deity of children. "These are the resting places of my mother's first two children. One died shortly after it was born. The other, a younger brother, died at three years old of pneumonia. He was such a smart kid," she remembers.

The practice of setting out a Jizo statue to remember children who were stillborn or who died young is called *mizuko kuyo*.

"When my other brother, Eitaro, died sixteen years ago, we already had so many headstones that it was recommended to my mother that his ashes be interred in the ancestral gorinto pagoda. You can see Eitaro's *kaimyo* [Buddhist name the priest gives someone after their death] here. The inscription also says Eitaro died at sixty years old.

"When people were still buried on Shiraishi, the body was interred the day of the funeral. But with cremation, the family doesn't put the urn inside the tomb until the forty-ninth day."

As we walk back down the steps of the graveyard, she points to a cleared plot. "These people moved their family grave to the Busshari-to." Black plastic has been tamped down over the ground to stop weeds from growing.

We pass the area of the graveyard where Eiko is interred, and I ask Mimiko if she would like to see the war widow's marker.

"Her husband must have been given a good kaimyo if he died in the war," Mimiko says. "A soldier's kaimyo is longer than normal. Usually the wife would be given a longer one too."

But when we arrive at Eiko's grave, there is no Buddhist name written on the stone. Nor is there a *kaimyoban* plate that lists all the family members' Buddhist names. Instead, there's just a lonely grave with the real names of the three deceased people written on the front, along with the ages and dates of their passing. Mimiko inspects the back of the marker. "Eiko's son's name is written on the back of the stone showing that he built the tomb in Heisei 15 [2003]. His name is written in red to show he's still alive."

But there is no Jizo statue for the three-year-old daughter.

If the grave wasn't erected until 2003, where were the husband's and the three-year-old's ashes kept before then? And if Eiko's son had a sister born in 1944, was she his twin?

We walk back down the Bonsan Michi to the beach. Before I leave, Mimiko looks around and says, "Where's Ma-kun? He's supposed to be looking after the shop! Ah, he disappeared. Not again!"

Four Chinese Brides

"I CAME TO JAPAN carrying a dictionary!" says Shoko.

"I came here because I was introduced by Shoko," says Kiyomi.

"I was already married to Nori-kun and living here." says Shoko. "But Hiroshi wasn't married yet, so I introduced him to Kiyomi."

"But how did you first come here, Shoko?" I ask. I remember her arrival, about a year after mine, which meant that the island, with a Chinese and an American resident, was now truly "international." All the girls came with Chinese names, but since they were a challenge for the Japanese residents to pronounce, they chose new Japanese names to be used in their adopted country.

"One of my friends in China owned a dating agency there that also did introductions overseas. So they put me in touch with Nori-kun. He actually came to China to meet me!" replies Shoko.

"I never thought I'd live abroad," says Kiyomi. "But I heard about the possibility of coming to Japan through Shoko and I thought it must be a nice place. So I came!" She gives a capricious laugh.

"Kiyomi is my uncle's friend's daughter," says Shoko. "Yoshimi and I are cousins."

Yoshimi nods. "I'm one of two children. In China, my father worked in transportation, delivering goods by truck."

"My father was an elementary school teacher," says Shoko. "My mother worked in a supermarket. I'm one of two children too."

The conversation bounces around the table like a ping pong ball trapped in a handball court. It's a lively conversation not just because all these girls are good friends who came to Japan at around the same time, but because they're Chinese so don't share the inhibitions of Japanese women. No one defers to the other, there is no order of seniority, and to me, these four Chinese brides, as they are called, are a welcome jumble of enthusiasm.

"We're all from Guilin," says Yoshie, adding her voice to the conversation. "It's very famous for its scenery."

"Except for me," Kiyomi points out. "I'm from Nanning. It's a five or six hour bus ride south of Guilin. I'm the youngest of five children. My father and mother ran their own tofu company. Before that my mother used to sew and my father worked at the board of education."

"I'm one of five children too," says Yoshie.

"At first my parents were a little concerned about me coming to Japan," says Shoko. "But after they came to visit me on Shiraishi they felt a lot better about me being here."

"Before I came to Japan, I was a little worried," Yoshie recalls. "I only knew about the wars so I thought that people might be mean to me or steal things. But after I came, nothing happened at all and I realized that my ideas, what I see on TV, and the reality of Japan are all different things. Even though Japan lost the war, I think the people worked really hard to overcome that. Japanese people are very patriotic, especially the older people. They really love their country so they worked hard to remake it into a good place."

Shoko jumps in. "A long time ago, there was a TV show called *Tokyo Love Story* that was popular in China. Everyone's image of Japan is Tokyo with all the buildings. They can't imagine the Japanese countryside. So when I came here everyone was surprised. I don't think many Chinese usually want to go to the countryside."

"But I like it here," says Kiyomi. "The countryside is fine with me. I don't want to go to Tokyo." She grimaces at the thought.

"My relatives wanted to know if everyone in Japan wore a kimono every day!" laughs Shoko.

These wives, full of adventure, were part of a Chinese diaspora of women looking to do something wild, exciting, even cutting edge. So they settled down in a foreign country where they'd be challenged, independent, and unique. They each married a local fisherman, learned Japanese on their own, and had two or three children. Now they are enjoying more free time, since most of their kids are in university on the mainland.

"If it hadn't been for me, none of these girls would have come here because they wouldn't have known anyone in Japan," says Shoko.

"Is it normal to use a go-between in China?" I ask.

"If there's a go-between, it's easier to meet someone," says Yoshie.

I mull this over for a while. "Well, I can't imagine any of my single friends in the US coming to Japan to get married and live on a small island just because I can introduce them to a cute, single guy."

"That's because people are happy in America," says Shoko. "But when we came to Japan twenty years ago, lots of Chinese people were leaving to go other places. Now, China has gotten much better and probably no one wants to leave. Hardly any brides come to Japan anymore. But in our time, we wanted to go do something different, something great!"

"I want to travel more," says Yoshie. "I want to go to America! And to Greece!"

"My daughter is at university in Okinawa," says Shoko. "But someday I want to go to Las Vegas!"

All the women help their husbands with their fishing jobs and some have additional work helping out elsewhere on the island.

"Three days a week, I work making bento-box lunches and delivering them to the elderly people on the island," says Kiyomi.

"Shoko and I work sewing for Hikino-san," says Yoshie.

"I don't know how to sew!" exclaims Yoshimi. "I'm busy enough with my two daughters and helping my husband. My daughters commute to high school on the mainland."

When I ask them what they don't like about Japan, they suddenly become quiet, not sure if they want to share their views with me. Finally, Shoko speaks.

"Nowadays even in China, everyone knows what's happening in the world. People are always putting their opinions on social media. China isn't like it was before: it's free now. The Chinese use social media when they don't agree with what their country is doing. We can get all the news about our home country even in Japan now."

"The problem with the news in Japan is that they only say bad things about China," adds Yoshie. "But every country has good things and bad things, so I wish they wouldn't concentrate on only the bad parts. China and Japan haven't always gotten along in the past, but if you concentrate on that, nothing will ever change. And the young people hear all this too and it affects how they think of relations, including those in the future."

❋ ❋ ❋

Hardly able to get a question in the last time I interviewed the four women, I decide on a new tactic. I invite the capricious Kiyomi to my house for coffee and cake so I can ask her a few more questions.

"My real name is Jie. It's difficult for Japanese people to say Jie, so I changed it to Kiyomi. I didn't have a wedding, per se. In China we had a celebration, but I just wore a nice skirt and he wore a suit. Then when I came to the island, we had a small get-together at the Fishermen's Union and a party at the Otafuku Bekkan inn.

"My job is to help my husband with the fish. In the summer, from April to November, the trawlers go out at night. They come back sometime between midnight and three in the morning depending on how many fish they catch. In winter, from December to March, we don't catch as many fish, and the trawlers go out during the day because it's warmer. It's a little easier for me then because I don't have to get up in the middle of the night."

When I start asking Kiyomi more of the details about fishing and the sea, she says, "Let me call my husband and ask him to come over." She dials the number on her mobile phone and turns on the speaker. "Hiroshi, Amy wants to know about fishing, can you come over to her house?"

"Not now, I'm hanging out the laundry," he says.

"That's okay, just come over when you're finished."

Soon, her husband enters the house and we're all sitting around drinking coffee and eating cake.

"What exactly do you do, Kiyomi, when you meet your husband at the dock?" I inquire.

"When the trawlers come back, all the wives go down to meet their partners on the pontoon in front of the Fishermen's Union.

The other wives get there before me because I'm not good at getting up in the middle of the night, so I'm usually the last one. We help our husbands sort the catch. I sort each type into a different wooden box—tonguefish, sea bass, red snapper, prawns and crab. I also ice down the fish. I get the ice from that huge ice maker next to the main building. Then we load them on to the *namasen*, the boat that takes everyone's fish into the market on the mainland. It's a lot of work and takes a few hours."

"One person could do the job," adds Hiroshi, "but it's a lot easier if you have someone to help. I know it's hard to be a fisherman's wife, but I'm glad she's so willing to give me a hand."

"How has fishing changed over the years?" I ask.

"There's not so much food left in the sea for the fish to eat, so the catch numbers are way down," Hiroshi replies. "These days in the winter, we're mostly trawling for crabs and mantis shrimp but there aren't so many of those around anymore. Before we used to catch big crustaceans in winter. Nowadays we don't catch anything like that. They're always small."

"Why do you think that is?"

"I'm not sure but one thing is that there are fewer places for fish to lay eggs. There is a lot of reclaimed land around here. There's the large area that was filled in to connect Konoshima Island to the mainland, and then there's the steel factory across the way. Before they filled in the sea to put in the factory, there were so many fishing nets you couldn't even get a big boat through."

"Sand was brought in from China to make Shiraishi Beach wider too," I add.

"You know, we used to have a natural beach there. When I was a child, it was full of seagrass on the bottom. Now there's hardly any. That's because those imported sand grains are too small. They gradually get carried back out to sea with the tide, so the seagrass has nothing to hold on to and it can't establish itself. Even though there are fewer and fewer fishermen, the population of fish hasn't increased, so something's wrong."

"The garbage in the sea doesn't help," I venture.

"There used to be a lot more garbage from the fishermen themselves. They used to throw absolutely everything into the sea! Even now some of the fishermen here on this island dump their fishing equipment. If you go even just a little further beyond the beach, you'll find leftover equipment from seaweed and oyster farming. If they're using it, that's okay, but once they abandon it, then that's garbage." Hiroshi points out that the red snapper seem to be doing better than before, referring to the fact that there are always some fish who benefit from adverse sea conditions. Just not most.

"Fishing seems dangerous," I say. "I know we lost a fisherman here many years ago."

The other fishermen knew something was wrong when they noticed a fishing boat circling with no one at the helm. In the wee hours of the morning, I watched as the other fishers towed his boat back into the port.

"You're remembering Noh-san," says Kiyomi.

"Noh-san slipped and got his hand stuck in the net roller drum used to bring the trawling net up," says Hiroshi. "His son came to identify the body and said that it had sliced him all the way up to his neck. Recently, a twenty-year-old fisherman from Kitagi Island died, and near Yorishima, a guy got caught in the drum of the net roller. It's almost always the drum, because even if you hit the emergency switch, it can't always stop in time. I know some fishers who take their wife or older son out trawling with them, but most of us on Shiraishi go out alone. But I'm not sure if fishing is any more dangerous than other jobs though."

The Dance Director

THE MAIN EVENT of the summer is the festival of the dead, called Bon or Obon, a time when the souls of the ancestors return to the island. A special fire is kindled in front of the Bussharito stupa to help guide the souls home, and it is believed that the jovial atmosphere of homecoming is enjoyed by family members both living and dead.

Kawata-san, the Director of the Shiraishi Bon Dance, is a small, fit man who walks lightly and carries a big smile. He's meeting me on the beach today to tell me about the history of the dance, a requiem for the dead that is performed annually during this summer festival.

"I came back to the island in Heisei 15 [2003] when I retired. My mother was still living here then. She was about ninety when I came back and she lived to a hundred. I took care of her the whole time. I'm still young—only seventy-seven. I took over as the director of the dance after Tadanori-san. It's been four or five years since he died, so that's how long I've been doing it.

"No one really knows for sure when the Shiraishi Bon Dance started but according to our folklore it was in the Kamakura period immediately following the Genpei War [1180 to 1185]. Two clans, the Heike [also called Taira] and the Genji [also called Minamoto], battled for control of all of Japan. Many of these battles took place in the Seto Inland Sea, and one of them was fought near here at Mizushima," he says, gesturing to a parcel of land on the coast of Honshu, visible from Shiraishi Island.

During the naval battle at Mizushima, the Genji and Heike warriors confronted each other in hand-to-hand combat by boarding each other's boats. Many of the warriors on both sides were wounded or killed and fell overboard. These corpses rode on the Inland Sea tides and washed up on the shores of nearby islands. On Shiraishi, warriors' bodies were found in three places: Kamiura Beach, the point of Ikenohara, and Yamori Beach, the latter meaning "arrow mound," named for the number of arrow-pierced bodies that were found there. The Bon dance is believed to appease their souls.

"When I learned the dance as a child, there was no kindergarten here yet," Mr. Kawata says, referring to the fact that for years now the local children learn the dance starting in kindergarten and continue practicing it through junior high. "We never learned the dance in school. Instead, it was passed down from the elders to us children."

Dance Director

"When I came back to the island I started going to Shiraishi Bon Dance practices with other islanders. The dance performance is for the repose of the souls of the Heike warriors who died in the naval battle of Mizushima, but we also include the fallen Genji warriors.

"It's an unusual Bon dance because it includes thirteen separate styles that all happen simultaneously in a big circle. Now we perform just six of those original thirteen, seven if you include the *burabura* dance which is so easy anyone can do it. As the island population has decreased, so have the number of styles. There just aren't enough people to have groups dancing all thirteen parts anymore. When I was a child though, we did all of them. And we danced late into the night and early into the next morning during the four days of the Bon festival.

"In 1976, the dance became an Intangible Folk Cultural Property not just because of its long history, but because it includes a song, a traditional Japanese *taiko* drum, and various styles of dance performed at the same time. Most other Bon dances are not so complicated. The original meaning of Bon is to call the dead spirits back for four days to mingle and have fun with us, and then to see them off at the end of that period. So for Bon on Shiraishi, we celebrate the spirits of our ancestors and include those who died in the Genpei War, thus the souls of our forefathers and those of the warriors become one. We dance for the glory of all of their spirits. Then we send our ancestors off by lighting candles for each family and float them out to sea. Of course, the warriors' souls are included. This is our long tradition."

The Future of the Shiraishi Bon Dance

"We used to perform the dance over where the community center is now, but when I was a child, that was a beach! When they put the ring road around the island, they also reclaimed that beach area and built the community center.

"I don't know what will happen to the Shiraishi dance from here on. We don't have a big enough population to continue the tradition. Every area in Japan has a Bon dance, but because ours is an Intangible Folk Cultural Property it carries a lot of weight. So we can't quit doing it just because we don't have enough people. The saddest thing is that the elementary school closed last year and next year the junior high school will close. There's no chance to continue the tradition without children inheriting it.

"So it's a matter of who can manage it from here on. In Kasaoka City right now they're forming a group to practice the dance once or twice a month. Some of the participants are high school students who are researching the dance and giving presentations, so the city thinks this might be one way to help preserve the tradition. If you don't make something a characteristic of your area, then people will forget it exists.

"These days, Japanese people have so many famous places to go. There's even modern art on some of the islands! So people know more about the new things, and less about the old. If they take the time to look up their own history, they'll find out about the Genpei War and the Shiraishi Bon Dance. But even then, they'd have to sort through a lot of Japanese history to find us!" He laughs at the absurdity of a country with such a long history that most of it cannot even be remembered.

"At Dan'noura, where the ultimate sea battle determined the victors of the Genpei War, there's an annual festival which brings in a lot of tourists. There's a Nasu no Yoichi festival as well, which recounts a famous scene from *The Tale of the Heike*. Eiheiji Temple in Fukui Prefecture celebrates the Heike general Taira no Kiyomori. We need to make something great here on Shiraishi too, so people will think to come. We need to weave together our history into a story, combining the temple, the Shiraishi dance and the history of the island. I think it's not too late to do something for Shiraishi Island."

I'm intrigued by Mr. Kawata's suggestions that make this conversation end on a high note. But there's just one more question I want to ask this man.

"What's the biggest difference between young people now and when you were growing up?"

He thinks for a while before speaking. "Young people don't know history. I remember the bombing of Fukuyama during World War II, even though I was only four years old. Why did they do such a thing, I wondered. The government makes decisions, but those decisions have nothing to do with the people. So that was a valuable lesson I learned when I was young.

"I understand why people live in more convenient places but if you live where life is too easy, you'll forget the old ways. You won't keep in mind the things your parents and grandparents taught you. You should at least try to keep the best parts of tradition.

"When I was young, I envied those living in the cities, but now I wonder why so many people would want to live there! These days, I think going into the city is a bother. You need transportation to get around, and it's hot. It's fine to go into the big smoke once or twice a month, to keep up with things. But if you wait and don't go for a year, everything has already changed. You don't know where anything is anymore.

"I prefer the island these days. I can walk everywhere I need to go. And when you get old and senile here, you don't need to worry. People will just help you. No one would ever do you any harm.

"It would be nice if we could think of ways to live independently here and not be tied to jobs in the cities. It's nice to live in a quiet place."

From my house on the port I have a clear view of Tomiyama Hill where people will come back to pray at their family tombs for Obon. The granite pillars creep down the hillside and I can even see Eiko's grave from here. As the night darkens, my eye is on the lookout for ghosts and *hitodama* fireballs, but all I see is the twinkling of moonbeams bouncing off the pointy monoliths and hat-topped pagoda tombstones.

As the tide begins to slip out of the port, the floating docks creak in the bunting of water riplets. As I drift off to sleep, the plangent cry of a gray heron pierces the night.

Keeper of the Graves

WHEN I AWAKE, I can see small specks of black moving around Tomiyama Hill like fleas on a dog's back. It's the start of the four-day Bon festival of the dead and people are up early to visit the graves.

Purple clouds scud across the sky as I walk up the Bonsan Michi path from this side of the port. The elderly have left their bicycles and pushcarts at the bottom of Tomiyama Hill while they struggle up the steps leading to the top, the lofty home of the dead.

I start the gradual climb up the long, wide concrete stairs, which are constructed so that each step is a few paces wide. The aroma of sweet incense lures me on. At the crest, the cemetery spreads out wide on both sides before the road descends to the beach and Mimiko's beach shack on the other side. Lengths of pampas fronds stir in the onshore breeze. Cicadas softly chirr.

The cemetery is effulgent, as people busily care for their ancestral graves. They flank the tombstones with fresh green *shikibi* branches or pine boughs and flowers. The usually drab gray stones burst with the resplendent colors of zinnias, cockscomb and chrysanthemums. People are gay with laughter as they call over to each other from the rows of headstones, and knot up in small groups to talk. Tea kettles and special plastic buckets are filled with water from the spigots along the road. Some scrub down the tall cylindric personifications of their loved ones, while others stand pensively in front of the pillars, hands together in prayer. Incense is lit and water is left in a small cup on the plinth: incense to create a special atmosphere for prayer, water so the deceased may quench their thirst. Always, the water.

Among the lanes of tall pillars, someone has even thought to put some leafed branches at the Heike memorial, erected as a tribute to the November 1183 battle at Mizushima. The monument, said to have been built in the early days of the Kamakura period (1192–

"The skiffs prowl out just as the black hues of night bleach into the ephemeral pastels of dawn." (A Day on the Port)

"We're sitting on the beach enjoying cans of beer at sunset." (The Cargo Ship Captain)

TOP: "I pass Turtle Rock on my way along the coastline. It's low tide, the only time you can see the stone's animal likeness." (A Quarryman)

LEFT: The temple holds a once-in-a-lifetime *shinzanshiki* ceremony when the Buddhist Priest officially hands over the temple to his son, the next generation. (The Buddhist Priest)

西浦海水浴場ニテ NHKノド自慢放送 昭和参拾年　*The Beach at Shiraishi Island 1955*

"[Until the 60s], our house and all the other beach businesses butted right up to the beach." (The Runaway)

A *mochi*-rice-cake-making celebration for a member's forty-second birthday, a *yakudoshi* bad luck year. (The Pufferfish Widow and Yakutoshi)

TOP: The mayor is carried to the top of Shiraishi in a palanquin. Tomiyama Hill is in the background.

ABOVE: "These are all my cousins. It's the New Year so everyone is wearing a kimono with the family crest on it." (The Doll Maker)

ABOVE: The Otafuku family at a send-off for Masagoro Amano, before he went to Manchuria with the Japanese Police Force in 1939. When he returned, he eventually opened the Amano Store and the Otafuku Ryokan inn. (A Reluctant Innkeeper)

LEFT: "Oh, what's that hulking in the corner? A life-size statue with a menacing face, wearing armor: it's a samurai!" (The Stone Bridge Lady)

ABOVE: Shinobu's doll festival display set out for Girls' Day. The imperial couple is at the top, the ox and carriage at the bottom. (Second Generation U-Turns)

LEFT: The words "Shiraishi Island" written in calligraphy by the Buddist Priest. (The Buddhist Priest)

ABOVE: "When my father had the Bussharito built in 1970, we allocated a place next to it to serve as a soldiers' resting place." (An Accidental Hermit)

LEFT: "We have a monument here at the temple for the war dead. It is engraved with the kanji *chukonhi*, a phrase that praises the loyal spirit of those who died in battle." (The Buddhist Priest)

A guardian Jizo watches over granite tombstones decoupled from their original graves. Included are soldiers' tombstones and *jizo* stones for children. (An Accidental Hermit)

Mr. Umakoshi, a seventh generation quarryman, built a stone wall around his house to protect it from typhoons. (A Quarryman)

"Wedding celebrations lasted four days back then. I had my hair made up in the *taka shimada* hairstyle of the day and I had to sleep with my head on a brick at night to keep my coiffure from unraveling."
(The Outsider)

The Heike memorial is the oldest commemorative stone on Tomiyama Hill and is a tribute to the warriors lost in the Genpei sea battles that ended in 1185. (Keeper of the Graves)

ABOVE: This photo of the prosperous fishers on Shiraishi Island dates from 1944.

LEFT AND BELOW: " 'When it was cold we fished in *donza*,' he says, referring to the padded fishing kimonos sewn with layers of cloth." (The Former Postmaster)

The Stone Bridge Lady as a child (front, second from right) with her family, the Haradas, at the renewal ceremony for the Kairyuji Temple Daishi-do building. Her mother and father are in the middle of the photo: he is wearing a white *kamishimo* (formal samurai outfit) and her mother has her hair set in the *marumage* style. This photo dates from the early Showa era.

ABOVE: "The original meaning of Bon is to call the dead spirits back for four days to mingle and have fun with us, and then to see them off at the end of that period." (The Dance Director)

LEFT: "The Ferry Captain, doubling as Tenrikyo priest, asks the *kami* (divine spirits) to protect Shiraishi Island, its beaches and surroundings." (The Ferry Captains Who Moonlight as Priests)

ABOVE: Some of the war widows from Shiraishi Island pose in front of Yasukuni Shrine in Tokyo, 1974. Yasukuni is where all the souls of the war dead are enshrined. War widows were called the Mothers of Yasukuni. Eiko is in front, fifth from left.

LEFT: Kimiya, left (Keeper of the Graves), and Amasaka-san, right (mother of Mimiko, the Runaway) stand together dressed in island festival wear, 1981.

Six-year-old Miwako, or Mi-chan, (center), wife of the Newspaper Delivery Man, stands ready to see off a ferry on the port, in 1955. The ritual of sending off important people, with ribbons stretched between the passenger and those standing on the pontoon, still exists today.

Mimiko dressed as an *omiko* shrine maiden,
at thirteen years old in 1957. (The Runaway)

1333), is also an ode to this island which, some say, also served as an Inland Sea battlefield. The monument, the oldest in the cemetery, is mottled with green lichen; its pagoda-like shape and crude edges pitted from the winds of time, and the passing of the years. This would have been the first memorial stone ever erected on Tomiyama Hill back when it was just a lone thicket of grass in nearly campestral surroundings. Who would have imagined that this monument would come to represent the dreams and ambitions of fallen warriors both then and now.

When I stop by Eiko's grave, I notice it has been looked after, arranged with its own simple boughs of shikibi. The stone has somehow warmed and softened with this splash of green, and seems to have gained some dignity. Yakutoshi told me that his mother, Katsuko, looks after Eiko's grave at Obon.

The chirruping cicadas grow louder as I climb further up the hill. There are some odd insects up here, real enthusiastic trillers, and I am lost in their infinite glee: *gee-gee-gee, gee-gee-gee*. In the morning freshness, the local grandmas are calling out "Good Morning!" from under their bonnets as they grunt their way up the steps. "Oh, lordy lordy!" a woman exclaims while plopping down on a graveside wall to rest.

I see my neighbor Kazu-chan chatting to someone and ask if she knows where Kio-chan's grave is. She doesn't.

Half-way up the mountain in the middle of the cemetery is the small wooden hut that Mimiko said the priest used for funerals in the days when people were buried. Inside is an image of the Buddhist saint Kobo Daishi. The door has been left open for the Bon festival period. Inside are small green tea cups for water and a decorative pot of sand for placing incense sticks. Three threads of smoke rise from the spot. The island bell rings 6 a.m.

Off to the side, a temporary structure has been built. Between four bamboo poles, a plank has been positioned to make a wooden altar. Called a *segaki dana*, this structure is set up to give solace to all the suffering spirits of the universe: dogs, cats, birds, trees, flowers, insects, even the lowly cockroach. It also feeds the "hungry ghosts," spirits with insatiable hunger. On its altar too, rests a small tea cup of water and an incense bowl.

As I climb further up, I pass a fisherman washing off his family grave. The water rushes off the polished surface in rivulets down onto orange Japanese lantern flowers.

Watanabe . . . Watanabe . . . where is Watanabe? I keep climbing.

I pass a vegetable garden, an odd site among tombs. But there it is.

As people flit from one grave to another, I realize some are taking care of multiple plots. I spot the Newspaper Delivery Man with his wife, Mi-chan, in front of a grave just two rows up. Mi-chan says, "Ohayo gozaimasu, Amy! What are you doing here?"

"Looking for Kio-chan's grave. You know, the stone miner who just passed away?"

"It's way up there at the top."

"Does it have a flag?" I ask, referring to the standard raised at Obon for a new grave.

"I'm not sure," she says.

I continue climbing.

"Ohayo gozaimasu!" I say to an elderly lady. "I'm looking for Kio-chan's grave."

"There aren't any flowers on it, but it's up there." She counts, "One, two, three, four rows up."

I ascend four more rows, until I'm at the top of the hill, at the edge of a clump of forest, when I see the grave marked "Watanabe." I pause in front of it and start thanking him for all the good times we had.

The elderly lady comes back, "Oh, I think you mean Kiofumi! This is his father, Kiomizu's grave. Kiofumi's is right there next to it."

I resume thanking Kio-chan rather than his father while the insects chant their own version of the sutras.

Kio-chan's grave is taller than me and is made of speckled, camel-colored stone. The vases on the sides are not simply drilled into the stone like most; instead, each vase is a separate piece, ground and smoothed into an elegant shape. The ossuary has the Watanabe family crest on it, carved into an exquisite white background. A lotus leaf on the plinth has been cut to match. The *kaimyoban* nameplate to the left has just three names on it, leaving plenty of space for other family members to follow. The Watanabes were stone miners who retired as business declined. It's odd that there is no flag, no flowers nor greenery in the expectant vases.

The screech of cicadas up here is deafening. A ship's long horn cuts through the din as thick as fog.

As I turn to walk back down Tomiyama Hill, the clear Inland Sea is spread out before me. I look across to the east and see Bikuni Rock, Myoken Shrine, and my house nestled below them on the breakwater. To the west are the distant Kibi Mountains on the mainland. On Tomiyama Hill, most graves face west, the direction of the sunset and of Amida Buddha's Paradise, where souls cross over into enlightenment. As I make my way carefully down the steep steps I hear an "Ohayo gozaimasu!" It's eighty-nine-year-old Kimiya, who lives in the house next to Mimiko on the beach. She's standing at the end of one of the cemetery rows. "I wonder if you could bring me that jug of water sitting there on the step." I'm only two steps above her and the jug is right at my feet.

"I know it's close, but for me it's quite far. Someone else brought it up here for me but she didn't know which row to place it in, and she put it up a little too high."

I carry the water down to her, but instead of taking it from me, she gestures for me to proceed down the row of graves. She tells me to go all the way to the end until I see a grave with the name Nishihara on it. I stop and wait for her.

"I'm so sorry to bother you with this," she says.

"I am happy to help you. Very happy actually."

"Arigato."

"I'm glad I can do something for someone," I say, then add in proper Japanese deprecation, "I'm quite useless."

"Oh, you are not useless," she says giving me an endearing one-tooth grin. She puffs and sits down. "Would you mind putting some water into this vase for me? Arigato. A little more, all the way until it's full."

She apologizes again. I tell her how much fun this is for me.

"Are you finished with that one yet? Have you put some water in there too?"

This means I'm not, and I haven't, so I look for what I've missed. Oh, there's a vase hidden behind the Jizo statue, so I pour water into it.

"You know, my son comes back but he's only here a day before he leaves again so he doesn't have time to help me." Then she says "Arigato, ne," in the quietest, sweetest whisper to herself.

"Shall I refill these jugs of water?"

"No, I'll take them home and bring them back when I come next time." She pauses for a moment. "I have to take a rest. Even though I come up here early, it's still hot."

Suddenly, she starts laughing, perhaps wondering for the first time why in the world I am in the graveyard. After all, it's a time to remember your ancestors, and I don't have any in Japan.

"Amy-san, whose grave were you visiting?"

"Watanabe Kio-chan's."

"Oh, did someone in his family die?"

"Kio-chan, in March."

"He did?"

"I heard about it only recently."

"I was in the hospital for two months, so I didn't know. Oh, that guy was so popular and fun!"

"Yes, yes!"

She reflects before intimating, in another whisper to herself, "So his wife is alone now."

We've lit the incense and are placing the sticks in the holders in front of each grave. I turn my back to reach the other graves. When I turn around again, she has rearranged the incense into clumps of two. She apologizes for correcting my poor incense form.

"Please, teach me," I plead.

"Stand two long sticks together here. There are eight sticks in this other bundle, so I thought I'd burn them all together." She brings out a paper matchbox and I strike the sulfur tips against the box.

"Just put those sticks in the bowl here," she says. "Put the other two way back there." The hidden grave again.

She is pensive. "That's the first I'd heard of Kio-chan having passed away," she says, in her soft voice. "Oh, dear." Then she continues to instruct her acolyte: "Please place a stick in here too. Was Kio-chan ill?"

"I'm not sure," I say.

"Watanabe Kiofumi-san passed away . . ." she repeats to herself, deep in thought.

Hands clasped together, she begins reciting the Heart Sutra. At first it's like a child singing out of tune and trying to remember, but gradually the chant starts rolling smoothly. Her own lilt indicates how comforted she is by the familiarity of the sounds. Her mouth cradles each word:

> The material world does not differ from emptiness.
> Emptiness does not differ from the material world.
> The material world is itself emptiness.
> Emptiness is itself the material world.

When she slows down, I know she is approaching the end of the sutra:

> Passed, passed,
> Passed to the other shore,
> We have all passed
> To purest enlightenment.

Then she wavers her voice while drawing out the last elongated coda *hanyaaaa shinnnngyo*, as if she doesn't want to let it go.

Finally, she divulges her appreciations aloud, "Thank you for giving me money, thank you for my health and thank you for finding this sister here in the graveyard who has done so many things for me today."

She turns to me, "Thank you for today, na? Arigato. It's tough getting old, you know. My husband Hayata died three years ago, Heisei 29 [2017], in January. This is the *honke* [main household] grave. No one else is still alive from his family. This is his brother here," she says referring to the obelisk. "He was young when he died in the war. Sankichi was his name. He died in the Philippines, Luzon. See? It's engraved here on the shaft." Chinese characters cascade down the side of the pillar telling the brief story of a man's final moments: the day, the place.

We leave the row of graves and make our way down the steps, slowly, stopping twice to rest by leaning against a grave. Earlier in the morning, Kimiya had left her cane at the bottom of the steps in order to free her hands to carry the offerings up to the graves. As we continue down the roughly laid stone steps, I clasp her warm bony hand and it rests in mine like a delicate little bird.

"These people live in Osaka, but they don't come back anymore," she says, pointing to a grave plot consumed by weeds. Then she scans the hill and remarks, "Look at all the flowers. The graves are really pretty at Obon, ne?"

At the bottom, she retrieves her stave and asks me to fill one of the jugs with water as we pass the tap.

"Ohayo gozaimasu," say the people walking past, not all of them familiar faces. Many people return to the island only at Obon to take care of their family graves. I'm happy to fill the jug for her, and even happier no one has to carry buckets of water up to these heights the way the Stone Bridge Lady did in her day.

When we start down the Bonsan Michi back towards her house on the beach, Kimiya tells me to take a left into the lower grave-yard on the opposite side. I enter the row. "Go straight. Keep going straight." Oh, so many Nishiharas!

"My immediate family is down here. This is a convenient place, right behind my house, so I can come anytime. But the ancestral graves way up there, not so much. Just put the jug of water here, next to my brother's wife's grave so I have it the next time I come. Arigato."

As we head back out onto the Bonsan Michi, a passerby says, "Ohayo gozaimasu," from under a bonnet. The woman is wearing a smock, long sleeves and gloves, and she's cradling a large covered box so full, the lid looks as if it will slide off.

"Oh, it's Kio-chan's wife!" says Kimiya, so she approaches her. "I just heard about your husband. When Amy told me Kio-chan had passed away I was so surprised. I was in the hospital two months because of a bad back and only returned to the island in March."

Mrs. Watanabe explains that Kio-chan had been sick. "There was nothing that could be done. He was in so much pain."

"When Hayata died, I didn't want to see anyone," Kimiya confides to her. "I didn't even want to go outside. I understand how you feel. Time will help, but even then there will be times when you remember and it will all rush back at you. Please take care of yourself."

Now I realize that inside Mrs. Watanabe's box are the flag, flowers and offerings for Kio-chan's grave. Once we've exchanged blessings, I walk with Kimiya back to her house.

"It's so hard when someone passes away," she says to me. "And Kio-chan was younger than me."

The Octopus Hunter

HIRO MEETS ME in front of his family's seafood restaurant on the beach, where a ceramic octopus pot and an old glass fishing buoy serve as decor. At forty, Hiro is the youngest fisherman on Shiraishi Island and just one of two octopus hunters left. He admits it's a lonely job these days compared to that of his predecessors, who combined forces to bring the island large catches and profits. He supplements his income with a beachside tent in the summertime where he rents out spaces to beachgoers. His wife, Saki, is also from Shiraishi but they recently moved to the mainland so the kids could go to school. With one child in kindergarten, one ready for nursery school and a newborn, it was much easier for them to move to the mainland and have the husband commute to Shiraishi, than to have the small children going back and forth. So now Hiro comes from the mainland to work where he used to live.

"Octopus pots used to be made from terracotta. But nowadays, they're made of durable plastic that is much lighter and doesn't break as easily. They're also weighted on the bottom," he says.

The fishermen tie the pots at intervals along a rope and lay them along the seabed like a string of pearls. The octopods snuggle into these dark crevices at night, only to have their dreams dashed when the Octopus Hunter evicts them into his boat in the early morning when the sun is still low and the moon high.

"Those blue glass buoys were used in gill-fishing," Hiro tells me, but nowadays they've been replaced with the black plastic buoys that can be seen bobbing on the sunlit surface almost anywhere in the Inland Sea. Whereas the old glass globes were secured inside small nets and then tied to the stationary fishing nets, these durable plastic ones have tabs built into their design to which the nets are tied.

Hiro first moved away from the island in elementary school

when his parents divorced. His mother took him and his brother to Tokyo with her. In the summer of 2003, his older brother decided to come back to visit their father, whom neither of them had seen in over a decade.

His brother had such a good time during his few weeks on the island that he invited some Tokyo friends to come down to visit. One evening, he and his friends decided to go to the mainland for some nightlife. The brother didn't have a boat license but one of the other young guys did, so they borrowed a boat from one of the fishermen. It was already dark when they left. As they motored between Konoshima and Takashima islands, the brother realized he had forgotten his cell phone. So they turned around to go back and get it. It must have been low tide then because when they turned the boat in a big semi-circle the boat ran up onto rocks. The passengers were all thrown from the boat. The guy who was piloting the boat, who suffered a broken arm, swam around for a while in the dark, eventually ending up on the shore of Takashima. The other friend also found his way to a beach. But the older brother was nowhere.

Their father, a diver, spent the next two days looking for his son on the bottom of the sea. Even he could not find him.

By now, the ex-wife and Hiro had come down from Tokyo to join the search. After three days, a call arrived early in the morning from Takashima. A fisherman had found a body floating in the water.

"It was the first time I had been back to the island since elementary school," says Hiro, "and to tell the truth, I didn't remember that much about the island, and I don't think I would have come back to Shiraishi if it hadn't been for my brother's accident. I had been working in a restaurant in the city and I still had a younger brother living at home. After we had the funeral in Tokyo, I brought the ashes back here and we scattered them in the sea. At that time, I called my mother in Tokyo and told her I wasn't going back to the city."

The next thing Hiro had to do was find a job here. And thus he decided that stalking octopi was his destiny. He procured a modest hand-me-down fishing boat and borrowed octopus pots from the Fishermen's Union. Shortly after that, he met Saki and now they have three children. In the summer he stays on the island, and in the winter or between octopus seasons, he stays with his family on the mainland.

The Octopus Hunter says he'll eventually take over his father's restaurant. "I try to respect the traditions and hang on to the regular customers who have been loyal all these years. I'll change things, but only very slowly." He's optimistic about the future.

"Right now the most important thing is to spend as much time as possible with my kids. Parenting styles are different these days. My father is old school. I don't have any memories of doing anything with my Dad when I was young. He was always working. I want to be a different kind of father."

Hiro feels a strong affinity with the island now. "Even though my kids have moved to the mainland, I want them to know and value Shiraishi so they'll always come back."

Second Generation U-Turns

THE SUN is just setting over the mountain, its crepuscular rays breaking through clouds as I cut across the flat plain of reclaimed land behind the breakwater. This flat area is comfortable and predictable, stretching almost all the way to Torinokuchi on the other side of the island. The fertile soil on either side of the road is where many locals keep immaculate market gardens. With the concrete strip, the elderly can easily access their garden plots and wheel harvests home in handcarts. The one-lane road is also used by cars but since there isn't much need for a vehicle on our island, it is often used as a promenade for morning and evening strolls. As I make my way down the road away from the port, the calls of herons and seagulls fade away and the trees ring with the birdsong of orange-bellied *jobitaki* and green-bodied "white-eyes," the latter named for the white circle around their eyes.

There is one particularly large and well-cared for garden that catches my eye. The rows are plowed neatly like thick corduroy. Each long puffy mound is sprouting new greens: young spinach and *endo* beans; a line of tufted carrot sprigs that give way to rubbery tipped onions; and an entire row of frowsy-headed daikon radishes. Finger-leafed watermelon vines crawl down their own humps. Between these rows of watermelon stands a blue-patterned cloth, wrapped with a white sheet of pleats, topped with a white bonnet, inside of which is the smiling face of a very old lady.

She looks up at me on my parapet and smiles, then walks over to the concrete steps that lead out of her veggie plot. She's a tiny creature wearing white sneakers with velcro closures and iris blue *mompe* pants. She walks nimbly up the stairs. I don't know who this lady is, but it doesn't matter. She's going to tell me.

"I wake up at eight o'clock every morning, have a leisurely breakfast and come out to the garden for an hour or two every day to weed. I like weeding!" she says with great enthusiasm. Then she surprises me by saying, "I talked you once at the Bussharito festival when I was serving sweet sake to devotees." I try to jog my brain. It's humbling that this ancient remembers something I had long forgotten.

"I thought I'd give up the garden this year because of the growing numbers of wild boar. But then I thought if I don't do anything, and just sit around at home, I'll waste away. So I decided to carry on. I'm ninety-four and come from Sanagi Island, in Kagawa Prefecture. My husband, Kikunosuke, is from here. He used to go fishing over in Shikoku and I met him there. Then he asked me to come be his wife. It was fate. I was twenty-three years old when I came here."

"Have you lived in Shiraishi since you were twenty-three?" I ask.

"My husband couldn't make a living fishing, so we left Shiraishi and moved to Osaka where Kikunosuke worked on a big boat. While living in Osaka, I gave birth to four children: three girls and one boy. After my husband retired, we came back to Shiraishi. He started fishing again but just catching small fish. We used to go fishing together. But I prefer meat over fish. I always eat beef in the evenings. I'd never had a garden before I came to Shiraishi, but now I've become a pro! I even have another one up on the mountain.

"Kikunosuke has been gone for about five years now. He used to love going to the festivals and he always had a good time. My son is still in Osaka but is retired now. I have a daughter in Osaka too, another in Kurashiki, and one on the island."

"One of your daughters lives here?"

"Yes, don't you know Shinobu?"

"Ah, you're Shinobu's mother, Mrs. Harada. I'm going to see Shinobu tomorrow!"

As the evening deepens into night, the old lady heads back down the stairs to put her hoe and hand-plow into a little shed next to her veggie patch. She makes the pilgrimage back and forth from house to garden twice a day: once in the fresh hours of the morning, and again in the cool hours of evening, walking about a mile a day.

❀ ❀ ❀

"Shinobu, I met your mother yesterday."

"Yes, she told me! Come on in."

I take my shoes off in the entryway before stepping up onto the floor of their house. Like most island houses, it is larger and roomier than the modern houses on the mainland.

"I didn't know your mother was on the island. She lives alone?"

"Yes, she makes her own breakfast and lunch but I go over to cook dinner with her every night. She likes to cook though. She lives in the house across from Panken."

"Oh, in that big house?"

I sit on the floor at the traditional low table, next to where her husband, Takanori, is already sitting. There is something intimate and equalizing about sitting together on the floor around a knee-high Japanese tea table

Shinobu and Takanori are U-Turns—the term used for people who leave the island then return. First Shinobu's mother and father came back to the island, then Shinobu did, making them second generation U-Turns. They retired and moved back to the island four years ago from just across the sea in Fukuyama. They love their ancestral home.

"I worked at the steel factory over there for forty years," Takanori tells me.

"I lived in Osaka, so I didn't go to school on Shiraishi," says Shinobu, placing tea and rice crackers on the table. "But I came on my summer vacations and that's when I met Takanori."

"I was working at the rowboat rental on the beach. I hooked her like a fish and reeled her in!" he says winding in an invisible fishing reel as fast as possible with his hands while laughing.

"And you're still happy together," I observe.

"The happiest!" he exclaims. "We came back here because we love Shiraishi!"

They are exemplary returnees. While some people come back to their hometown to simply retire, this couple has made it their mission to improve the island so that they can encourage more returnees to revisit the life here. They exude a sense of gratitude for island life.

"We have five children," he says, "but all of them live on the mainland now."

Saki is their youngest daughter, who married the Octopus Hunter. Takanori leaves the table and shortly returns carrying two pictures in large wooden frames.

Realizing her husband has just grabbed the photos off the wall, Shinobu yells "Dust! Dust!" while snatching a tissue from the box on the table. The husband wipes down the glass and frame, although not a speck of dirt shows on the tissue paper. In the photo, the family is standing together in front of the house we're inside now. He points out, among the relatives, a younger version of themselves with small children in their arms. One of the children is doll-like in a kimono, staring out from underneath the blunt bangs of her hair. This photo was taken at the New Year," he says, and identifies each family member. But the two youngest children, including their daughter Saki, weren't born yet. The back of the photo notes it was taken on New Year's Day thirty years earlier, in Showa 61 (1986).

The next picture is of Shinobu's father's eighty-eighth birthday. He and her mother are sitting on two chairs in the middle of a group of people. This photo was taken seven or eight years ago, they tell me, and I can now see what Shinobu's mother looks like without her bonnet. The father is wearing a fetching yellow outfit with a funky boat-shaped yellow hat. A person's eighty-eighth is special in Japan, and is called *beiju*. The kanji for eighty-eight in Japanese, when written vertically, looks similar to the ideogram for rice, so the family celebrates this special birthday with bowls of Japanese sticky white rice and the celebrant wears auspicious yellow, or gold. "He used to love the festivals," Shinobu said of her father. "At the Fall Festival, he'd sit inside our neighborhood *mikoshi* portable shrine and pound the *taiko* drum to the music as the neighbors pulled the mikoshi up to Shisha Shrine. He lived into his nineties. He had a good life," she says, satisfied.

"In the old days most extended families lived under one roof," she continues. "At one time there were nine to ten people per household.

Imagine it! The elementary school had six classes of fifty students each, and the junior high had three classes of fifty students, so four hundred and fifty students in all. Then they added the kindergarten."

"In those days," says Takanori, "people intermarried. As long as you're not closer than first cousins, it's safe to intermarry, so relatives were close in both distance and blood. Now people marry others from far away and we don't know anything about their families or who they are. We don't know their relatives so we don't share those close family connections anymore.

"Before, when everyone lived together, it wasn't always easy. The kids and parents would argue a lot. But that's good. People need to interact and learn things from each other and kids need to learn by interacting with various adults in the family.

"On Shiraishi there was no nursery school, so the kids who weren't of school age were looked after by their grandparents at home. And older brothers and sisters took care of the younger ones."

"But after the kindergarten and elementary school closed last year, our grandchildren couldn't stay on the island," laments Shinobu. This also means the grandkids don't have the benefit of spending more time with their grandparents.

"When we were young, each seaside house or beach shack would rake the sand in front of their place so the beach was always clean. It would be nice if people would get together even just once a month to clean the beach now. We picked up garbage this morning with our grandkids who are visiting for the weekend," she says.

Takanori takes a breath. "Amy, this is the first time you've come to our house. But here we are laughing and talking. This is the kind of thing people need to do more often. Neighbors should get together, say, once a month. Then, before they part again, they'll say 'What shall we do next time?' and plan it right then. This is how to strengthen community ties. That way there's always someone to help if you need it too."

Rural communities all over Japan struggle to stay relevant among their more iconoclastic children and grandchildren who value convenience over tradition. But traditional values are still at the core of much of Japanese culture. So last year Takanori, Shinobu and a few like-minded islanders came up with an event that would not only involve the retired people, but would also help keep traditions alive.

"Actually, it was my classmate's idea," says Takanori. "He and I have the same wedding anniversary. We both married our spouses on the exact same day forty years ago; me at the Otafuku Bekkan and him at the Nakanishiya. It was fate! So we always celebrate our anniversaries together."

"The idea," Shinobu says, steering the conversation back on track, "was that in March, in celebration of Girl's Day, we would hold a traditional Hina Matsuri Doll Festival exhibition. Over the ten-day period over three hundred people came to see it, even people from the mainland!"

The annual Hina Matsuri festival was observed in homes all over Japan until recently. Traditionally, when a female child is born, the grandparents buy her a Hina Doll display, which is taken out of the closet and exhibited for the week leading up to Girls' Day on March 3. The displays are large and can take up a good portion of a room in a small Japanese house. Seven tiered shelves are covered in red cloth, each containing a row of dolls in Heian-period court costumes. The top shelf is reserved for the emperor and empress figures robed in kimonos, sitting Japanese style on cushions, with gold folding screens stretched out behind them. The lower tiers of shelves exhibit the court retainers in descending order, concluding with the musicians, attendants and maids. The shelf at the bottom includes a miniature wooden chest representative of the container a girl would store her valuables in to take with her when she gets married. Two other miniatures—a nobleman's carriage and an ox to pull it—are to take the bride and her belongings to her new household.

Shinobu shows me photos on her cell phone. "All these traditional doll displays have been in closets for twenty years or more. What a shame not to display these fine works of art. It used to be that every family with female children put up these displays and neighbors would come around and visit each house. The host would serve sweet sake and special doll-festival treats after which the visitors would go off to visit the next house. One display is from ninety years ago that Danshi's wife had kept. We even made the newspaper! Of course, we all want to do it again next year.

"Island people are good about helping if you ask them. A group of women made sushi to serve to guests. Your neighbor Kazu-chan also came and pitched in—it was just like back in the old days when people had to help each other. When it was all finished, everyone said, 'Let's do it again!' People are so busy these days, but they should find the time to do these types of things. And look at these miniature figurines performing the Shiraishi Bon Dance. Okae, the Doll Maker created these. They should be sold at the ferry port! The culture is deep here on Shiraishi Island. We have to do something; It's a waste if we don't."

"I work at the ferry ticket office now," says her husband, "so I have an opportunity to talk to people and remind them to have fun. Especially the young people. When visitors come to the island, I ask them where they are going and if they say, 'We're going to hike in the mountain,' or 'We're going to see Armor Rock" [of interest to geologists] then I tell them to first go see the Doll Festival exhibition before they head up the mountain. So tourists get to see something they weren't expecting. It's important to introduce people to the special things on our island."

"It would be nice if more people would move back to the island and have this kind of fun," adds Shinobu. "We need to make it attractive for them to come back, so they know there is a community here waiting for them."

"I wish people would enjoy life more," laments her husband. "Next we're going to string up traditional carp flags for Children's Day. Even if all we do is sit under the carp streamers and drink sake and beer, everyone will have a great time. No one else plans these things except us. But it brings the community together and we all rediscover our friends and start to enjoy ourselves again.

"Now Saki and Hiro have moved to Fukuyama because the kindergarten and elementary school here closed. Our grandchildren come to visit because we're here but after we die, they won't come back if there is no family to visit. There'll just be an empty house. If

Saki comes back to live here, then it might be different. Her brothers and sisters and their kids will come back to see her. And she'll take care of the family graves. But if she doesn't come back, then the others might not come back either except once a year for the Bon festival. Shiraishi will be sad and lonely in the future."

✳ ✳ ✳

Walking to the beach via the Bonson Michi today, I run into Hide-ichiro, the Cargo Ship Captain, on Tomiyama Hill. He's holding a small aluminum tea pot without a lid, a box of incense and a sutra book. "It's the anniversary of my mother's death so I've just visited her grave," he says. "I almost forgot!"

I invite him to join me on the beach for a beer.

He puts down his tools near the water spigot and we walk down the road and settle into some beach chairs. Hideichiro rattles off the dates easily: "My father died on April 17, my grandfather May 1, and my grandmother May 20. Sometimes I visit the graves on the monthly anniversaries of those dates too. When I'm there, I refill the vases with water, light some sticks of incense and recite the Heart Sutra. I don't know it by rote so I need to use the sutra book. And I recite each sutra three times." He assumes the position: sitting up straight, touching his chin to his chest, hands folded together. With eyes closed he takes a deep breath and starts intoning the Heart Sutra:

> The material world does not differ from emptiness.
> Emptiness does not differ from the material world.
> The material world is itself emptiness.
> Emptiness is itself the material world.

Then he drops off into laughter. "When I was working on the boat, I couldn't go to funerals often, so I wasn't good with the sutras. But when my father-in-law's father died recently at ninety-seven, we had to go to the grave for the first seven days after the funeral and recite the sutras each visit.

"You know, the cemetery didn't used to look as prominent as it does now because not everyone had the money to put up a tombstone. Nowadays everyone has one, and sometimes they've replaced the old gravestones with new polished ones, so now the cemetery has such a presence the sun reflects off the stones!

"My grandmother was buried up there but my grandfather was cremated because by the time he died, they had built the crematorium in Kasaoka. But when I die, they can do whatever they want with my body. Even just scattering my ashes in the sea in front of my house is fine with me! Before, people had more faith. I believe there's something that happens to us after we die but as long as I've done nothing wrong, I'm not worried about what that fate might be."

As we look out at the sea, I'm regretting the waning summer. The school holidays are over, the tourists have gone and Mimiko will head back to Tokyo soon. I bemoan this last fact to Hideichiro.

"I remember Amasaka, a fish vendor," he says, recalling Mimiko's mother. "She sold whale, you know. In those days no one ate meat, only fish. You know where the road branches off at Haramatsu Store to go up to the temple? Amasaka would stand there and sell fish because that was an intersection of three roads. I remember this from when I was young."

I'm almost dozing off from the heat when Hideichiro says something that brings me to attention.

"I knew Mimiko's younger brother. His name was Eitaro. He fell in love with a woman and wanted to marry her. But in those days, you had to wait till your older siblings married before you could. There was a pecking order. But Eitaro's girlfriend grew weary of waiting and left him to marry someone else. He never got over the heart-break, and never married anyone else. He remained single his whole life. Eventually, when Amasaka needed elderly care, Eitaro came back to live with her and took a job on the ferry. Then he got sick. He died before his mother, in his *kanreki* year [sixty years old]."

As we're talking, a youth group is holding an event on the beach in front of the Otafuku inn. The activity is called *jibiki-ami*. It works like this: the Fish Trapper brings his boat up until it just noses the beach, then turns it about face in the other direction, towards the sea. While the boat idles, he stands at the stern and throws out the end of a long net to an adult standing on the beach. He shifts the boat into gear and, as he steers very, very slowly into a large arc, he lays the long fishing net into the water. The net has light weights strung across the bottom and small floats along the top to keep the net standing. He finishes the arc 50 yards (50 meters) down the beach and hands the other end of the long net to another adult. The net billows out in a semicircle from the shore.

The young people standing on the beach now split into two single-file lines of about twenty kids each. They all grasp an end of the net as if they're playing Tug of War. Both lines of kids start pulling on the net to bring it in. Each line walks backwards as their team pulls and pulls. The net is heavy, but they keep pulling. And pulling. When they've finally dragged the net back up onto the beach, they are treated to a bevy of unsuspecting fish that have been swept up in the net and are now flopping around on the sand. Hundreds of less desirable bait fish get caught but the kids have lassoed some big fish too. And some huge ones as well. This favorite beach pastime is topped off with a seafood barbecue prepared by the kitchen staff at the inn.

Noticing their catch, I say, "It seems like a lot of fish go to waste in that event. I'm sure they eat the big fish, but what happens to the hundreds of small ones that no one wants?

The Boat Captain takes a swig of his beer and says, "But with jibiki-ami, they put the fish into the net."

"What?"

"The Fish Trapper. He puts the fish in. He's my classmate."

"You've got to be kidding!"

"Surely you didn't think that with just one net thrown out there they could catch that many fish?" He gives a belly laugh.

"I did think that!" I'm still astonished, but also laughing now. "Do the kids know?"

"I doubt it. But when the Fish Trapper takes the net around in the semicircle with his boat, he's not just putting the net in, he's dropping big fish into it too."

"But years ago they didn't add fish did they?"

"Nah. But nowadays when people come to the island to do jibiki-ami, they have to make sure they catch a lot of fish to please them."

"Look, there's Hiroshi's boat," he says pointing to the horizon. Another trawler is close behind, and another. It's so quiet we can hear the soft sound of motors pushing them along. The boats form a line creeping across the blood-red sun setting over a metallic blue sea.

The lights from the steel factory across the water start sparkling in the twilight. We've lingered long enough and there is just a half hour of daylight left. We set off home along the Bonsan Michi.

As we crest Tomiyama Hill we pick up Hideichiro's teapot and tools at the water spigot, then I pull him to the side to have a look at Eiko's gravestone. "Oh yes, I know her son. He was a ferry captain and works in Shikoku."

He looks at the names etched on the grave: Shoichi Nakagawa, Eiko Nakagawa, Emiko Nakagawa.

"Eh? Strange," he says. He looks at the back of the grave, then at the names on the front again. "Ehhhh? That can't be!" Again, he hesitates. "They must've made a mistake," he finally says. "It says that Shoichi Nakagawa died in 1945. But that can't be. I have a friend who was in the same class as Eiko's son. My friend was born in 1954!"

Shortly after I moved into this house on the port, I replaced the frosted glass windows with clear panes, so that now I have panoramic views: kites circling above, ducks buoyant on the water's surface, and herons standing one-legged, fishing among the seagrass at low tide. I can see the seagulls lined up on the jetty, looking out toward the lighthouse and the sea.

This morning, I feel the usual slight trembling that passes through the house every time a tugboat chugs past the lighthouse. Except this time it's not a boat, it's the vibration of my mobile phone.

"Sorry to call so early," says Mimiko breathlessly. "I planned on going back to Tokyo tomorrow, but this morning I found a huge centipede in my futon! I won't be able to sleep tonight, so I've decided to leave today instead."

I drive over to Mimiko's beach shack and we load her suitcase, her two cats, and herself into my small Mitsubishi pickup truck. I drive her back to the port, past the small island where the sea goddess lives, to catch the 8 a.m. car ferry. At the pier I hand the suitcase over to the Ferry Captain who will send it on to Tokyo straight from the boat. When all the cars are loaded, Mimiko is the last to board. As I wave goodbye, she disappears behind the boat's rising loading ramp, unable to wave back because she is clutching a pet carrier in each hand, inside of which are her two cats Mimi and Eita, the latter named in memory of her deceased younger brother, Eitaro.

The Buddhist Priest

"I WAS BORN IN SHOWA 8 [1933], the same year as Emperor Aki-hito. My birth mother died when I was six years old. My father, also a Buddhist priest, remarried and had three more children: one boy and two girls. One of my sisters died young. My younger brother became a banker and lived in London for a long time. He's now retired, living near Tokyo. My younger sister moved to Tokyo too. So only I'm left here at the temple."

The priest and I are sitting in an improbable English-style garden at the island's Buddhist temple. It's a fine autumn day and when one of the last of the season's mosquitos whines past my ear, I am careful not to murder it in front of the priest across the table from me. His wife is off the island today at ikebana class and we're just passing the time at his house, the temple, in the garden graced with a jacaranda tree and a wrought-iron garden table pierced with a sun umbrella.

He is telling me how a soldier's tombstone can be distinguished from others because the top of its pillar has four triangular sides that come together at a point.

"It's like a sword," he says. "About 120 young men from this island have died in wars since the Meiji era began in 1868. But not all of them have these sword-tip graves."

It was a personal decision by the family to elect to have such a gravestone, but during the American Occupation, General MacArthur effectively banned the practice of using this shape on tombstones because it has a military connection.

"You know we have a monument here at the temple for the war dead. It is engraved with the kanji *chukonhi*, a phrase that praises the loyal spirit of those who died in battle. These monuments were destroyed all over Japan after the war. But here on Shiraishi Island, we resisted this effort and for that reason it still stands today, preserved as a part of our history. If you look closely at the tower, you can see where they started to fill in the engraved writing, the first step to disassembling it.

"I remember World War II very well. We elementary school students would walk with the island people forming a parade all the way to the harbor to see the soldiers off to war. There would be a ceremony, and the new recruits would give a parting speech. When the boat left, we all shouted, 'Banzai! Banzai!'"

There were about two thousand people living on Shiraishi Island then. "I didn't have any brothers or sisters yet, so I played by myself or with my friends. In 1944, when I was eleven, I heard about Japanese planes hiding on the backside of the island at Torinokuchi, so my friend and I went to see them. The pilots had dug airplane bunkers in the beach and they were sitting in the cockpits.

"Air attacks were very heavy at that time. There were air raids next door on Kitagi Island too, B-24 bombers. We could hear explosions on Kitagi and in Fukuyama City on the mainland. We were not bombed here on Shiraishi, maybe because the attacks took place at night. This is a small island with few lights. Kitagi is much bigger, so maybe they could see it better at night.

"We students had to dig foxholes so if the Americans attacked, we could hide there. We were afraid the school would be bombed. If the wooden schoolhouse caught fire, we would need to work quickly to put out the blaze, so we trained for this by forming a human chain and passing buckets of water from the well to the school. The first person picks up the bucket by the handle [he stands up and demonstrates] and passes it to the next kid who receives the bucket with his hands grasping the bottom. He passes it to the next child who takes the bucket by the handle and so on, all the way down the line. This is the fastest and most efficient way.

"We didn't have many clothes, not even socks, and food was scant. So even very little boys and girls went together into the mountains where we cultivated plots to grow sweet potatoes or radishes. We made salt from the seawater at the port where the Fishermen's Union is now, near your house. The system used to separate the salt from the water was to simply take sea water and sit it out to evaporate in the sun. We went down again and again to gather the crystallized salt left behind. Even on the mainland people made salt. They'd go to the seaside and take buckets of saltwater back to their house to make briny pickles.

"I remember as a small child watching Tetsumi's mother-in-law— you know, Tetsumi, the manager of the Otafuku inn—carrying tofu on a bamboo pole over the shoulder. It had two barrels hanging from it and they were full of liquid and tofu. She was a beautiful woman and her body was muscular from the hard work. I remember watching her, how hard she worked, and the pain on her face from the weight as she hoisted the heavy barrels onto her shoulders to take tofu across the island to the rock quarries to sell it to the workers. It really impressed me as a child.

"One day all us school boys were standing around when we saw a Japanese plane fly over our heads. It turned out to be our classmate's father! He buzzed over the island, dropped a letter down to his house, then tipped his wing in salutation and rejoined his airborne group. He survived the war and came back to Shiraishi when it was over.

"Another time, my friend came up to the temple to get me. He shouted, 'A plane has come! It's in the port now, in the water.' I said 'Liar!' And he said, 'No, really!' So we ran down the hill from the temple to the port. And sure enough, there was a plane floating inside the harbor! It had pontoons on it. I was astonished."

The priest's own father avoided conscription due to a problem with his lungs. But even he couldn't escape the tragedies of war: as the island's sole Buddhist priest, he had to perform memorials for the fallen soldiers. The fatalities increased markedly the longer the war dragged on.

"Were any Shiraishi people affected by the Hiroshima bombing?" I ask. Hiroshima City is 80 miles (125 kilometers) to the west.

"Hachiro Komiyama was in Hiroshima that day," the priest recalls. "He was carrying two buckets of water on the ends of a bamboo pole over his shoulder to take to his fishing boat. He saw a big flash of light, and was knocked into the sea. He was able to escape on his boat but as he hurried away, he watched flames roar up over the city. When he came back to Shiraishi, he told us this story. Later he found out he had radiation sickness. There was another islander who worked for the National Railroad at Hiroshima Station. That morning while the employees were doing their morning exercises outside, they saw that very big light. He also got radiation poisoning. They've passed on now."

"After the war ended, there were many American GI's on the mainland in Kasaoka. In front of the train station there were rows of bars and entertainment lounges for American soldiers that were off-limits to Japanese. I could hear the foreign music flowing out of the bars. It was the first time for me to hear jazz. Funny music, I thought."

A ship's horn blows: the last ferry of the day is entering the port. Although the harbor is half a mile away, the sound rolls up the mountainside to us like smoke from a fire. The priest's wife is returning from ikebana class and they will soon sit down to dinner, so I leave the English garden through the gate and walk down the same road people had taken to form a parade to the harbor to see the soldiers off to war.

I'm going through my desk drawer at home looking for an old photograph that surfaced in this house years ago. At the time, I had no idea what the meaning of the image was, but I feel I am beginning to understand.

I am amazed I have kept it so close at hand all these years, only having looked at it once or twice. When I find it, I place it on the desk in front of me.

Forty-eight matronly women are sitting for a memorial photo. They are all wearing the same type of short-sleeved Western-style dress, hemmed to just below the knee. Some of the dresses have patterns while some do not. Some of the women wear eye glasses, but most do not. They all have their hair tied back. The first row of women are seated on a bench, the second, third and fourth rows are standing on stairs. The somber atmosphere is encouraged by the sepia tone of the photo. The women have not been instructed to sit with their feet aligned in any certain direction. Some do the duchess slant to the right, some to the left, and others point their knees forward. All have their hands folded neatly on their laps, or on top of their purses. None are smiling. They stare out, expressionless.

The group is standing in front of propped-open cypress doors on which I can barely see the edges of a chrysanthemum crest. In the mist-like overexposure, a *torii* gate in the background frames a shrine at the end of a long walkway, the furthest focal point of the camera lens. In back of the torii gate, a two-tiered roof is visible, under which hangs a long horizontal curtain, split and gathered in the middle. From this drape dangles a white Shinto purification paper.

The bottom of the photo reads, in Japanese: Yasukuni Shrine, Showa 49, August 20. The photo was taken in 1974 just after the Bon festival of the dead.

These women are posing at the approach to the shrine in Tokyo where it is believed all the souls of Japan's war dead reside. The women are war widows.

The Doll Maker

"I USED TO SEW their tiny kimonos with scrap material," Okae says, referring to the miniature dolls, an inch-and-a-half (four centimeters) tall, that she makes by hand. "I knitted their sandals and parasols too. I used to make the figures with clay, but now I use resin, which I can mold into kimonos and then paint." The resin is scored to show the swaying of the kimono, the cut of the cloth when a dance step is taken, the pleats in a bow, or to make cords for the obi sash. The doll I'm looking at has a tuft of black cotton sewing threads for hair that juts out of a purple headscarf which blends into a light blue kimono with long sleeves. The kimono has three family crests along the back, and a red obi with white stripes. The doll holds a folding fan in her right hand. Her legs are slightly parted as she walks into the next stage of the Shiraishi Bon Dance.

"I've danced the Shiraishi dance many times of course, but stepping into that big circle of people is uncomfortable for me. So I make these dolls and I dance through them," Okae tells me.

I'm sitting in the Doll Maker's beautiful old Japanese house. Before my arrival, she prepared a black-and-white family photo and sketchbooks. "We were four children, all girls. I was in first grade when the war ended. When we heard the scream of the air-raid sirens, we were taken to the temple where we could hide under the camellia trees. If there were already too many people there, we'd build a shelter in the school sport's ground by digging a hole.

"We didn't even have textbooks at school until I was in second grade. In junior high I didn't have my own either, so I borrowed from senior students or my older cousins. I didn't go on to high school because I'm not very smart," she says with a laugh.

"My older sisters went to junior high, but at that time, they didn't have to go if they didn't want to. By the time I was that age,

140

the school was strict about attendance, so I had to go every day, even when it was raining! During the rainy season I'd walk to school in wooden *geta* sandals, then I'd wash my feet off when I arrived and change into straw sandals for inside. My grandfather made our straw sandals by hand.

"At the end of the war, we were all living hand to mouth. Because there were no jobs, lots of young people were still living at home on the island. We didn't have TVs or any form of entertainment, so we just talked and socialized for fun.

"There was a youth group that put on social dances once a week. I loved going! I dressed up in a bouffant skirt." She traces the shape of the puffy skirt on her body with her soft doll-maker's hands. "Everyone came to the dances: the temple priest, the doctor, the teacher from school and Nakanishiya's son who was a pilot. He would fly abroad but when he had time off he'd come back to visit and come to the dances." Then she frowns behind a smile and says, "But no one ever asked for my hand at the dance. The Buddhist priest wouldn't even look at me! I was always so embarrassed."

She laughs it off, but the child inside me feels the hurt.

Marriage

"Did you have an arranged marriage?" I ask.

"Mmm, not really," she says behind a smirk. Then she leans in close to tell me a secret. But first she puts her coffee cup down on the Bizen pottery saucer, letting the bottom of the cup scrape across the unglazed surface. She's clearly embarrassed about what she's about to say, but can hardly keep her secret in. She lowers her voice to a whisper, the smile never leaving her face. "Every night he came to my house!" she declared and pursed her lips. "In those days, we had no entertainment, so the boys would come over in the evening. He was the one who came every night!" she confides, referring to the practice of *yobai,* where boys would sneak into girls' houses at night to fool around, that I'd first heard about from Danshi, the Fish Trapper's Father.

"After I married I had my tiger child," she says, referring to the Chinese zodiac year in which her first son was born, 1962.

"My husband worked on a boat for a while then after that he delivered the mail. He wasn't planning on quitting the post office job, but there was a guy in our neighborhood who didn't have a job and was really struggling, so my husband gave him his job and took another as captain of the *namasen* boat that went to the fish markets. Once the fishers had sorted and loaded their catches, my husband had to deliver them to the mainland by four o'clock in the morning.

"When my husband fell ill, I'd take a small bucket and go fishing. I could catch about ten fish easily while he was still sleeping. Between the large rocks on the shore you can drop a line in and hole fish. The only bait I used was frozen krill I bought at the grocery store. When I brought the live fish back in the bucket, I'd cook them for my husband because fish were good for him and they're much better when they're fresh.

"Do you like *hijiki*?" she says, referring to the seaweed. "I'd go to the beach at seven in the morning and collect hijiki, but I tell you, catching fish was much more interesting. While I collected the hijiki off the rocks, the fish would jump out of the sand, so I'd pick them up. One time I came back with twenty of those fish! But as soon as the weather gets cold, they hide in the sand. So I'd dig into the sand and they'd wiggle and flip their tails. You gotta dig 'em out quickly before they escape back into the sea. See? These are the kinds of experiences you can have if you live into your eighties!

"I didn't start sketching until my husband fell sick," continues the eighty-three-year-old dilettante. "When he reached the point where he could only sit at the *kotatsu* table and watch TV, I wanted to be by his side, so I tried sketching while sitting at the kotatsu. That's when I realized I could draw! And I couldn't stop. I filled up three of these sketchbooks front to back! I used color pencils because just a regular pencil was kind of boring." She shows me her sketchbook: gardenia, camellia, hibiscus, a snail, the folk hero Momotaro, and *dango* sweets eaten while moon-viewing.

Future U-Turns

"Do you think your children will ever come back to the island?" I ask.

"All three of my kids want to come back. My daughter told her husband 'I'm going back to Shiraishi when I retire, what are you going to do?' Her husband says he'll stay in Yokohama, where he's from.

"When my son came back to visit from Nagoya last time he said, 'You know, they don't make houses like this anymore.' He really loves these old homes. He said this island house isn't worth that much on the real-estate market, but his house in Nagoya is worth quite a bit. So when he retires, he wants to sell the Nagoya house and move back here.

"My kids always come back for the Fall Festival. When the grand-kids were little they would ride inside the *mikoshi* portable shrine. You know, in the old days, women weren't allowed to touch the mikoshi, so we didn't pull it.

"Elementary school girls took turns being *omiko* dancers performing the purification rites at Shisha Shrine. We had so many students who wanted to be omiko, there was a lottery to choose who could participate. I hit it when I was in sixth grade. The dance is similar to *kagura*, a Shinto dance for the gods. The *oni* devil comes out, and they dance together."

The dance had been performed for hundreds of years, but as the island population decreased, there were fewer and fewer students to sustain the tradition. The lottery was made redundant, and five years ago, three omiko danced for the last time. That was the year the elementary school closed.

"These are my ancestors. This photo was taken eighty-five years ago, before I was born." It's a large black-and-white print. "You know the barber? I'm related to him. This photo was taken in front of his family home, where the barber shop is now. The original photo was very small but when my relative found it in her drawer, she had it enlarged. I was so surprised when it was made bigger—you could see everyone's facial features!

"These are my two elder sisters. This person here, my uncle, went to Hokkaido and married someone there so didn't come back except occasionally at the New Year. I just couldn't believe he moved to Hokkaido. It took so many days to get there. He never came back even once while the war was on. This is the only photo we have of him," she says wistfully.

"These are all my cousins. It's the New Year so everyone is wearing a kimono with the family crest on it. When I was a child, at the New Year my grandparents on my mother's side bought me all new clothes, from underwear on up! Since we only received new clothes once a year, those kimonos were so old and battered by the time the next New Year came around.

"This is the Stone Bridge Lady's father-in-law. Do you know the Former Postmaster? My mother's side of the family and his side of the family are cousins. And this here is the father of the guy who owned the Otafuku. The people who originally owned the Nakanishiya were my grandparents on my father's side."

My head is spinning.

"One of my sisters still lives on Shiraishi. You know Goro, the guy who walks with his wife in the evenings? That's my elder sister Katsue and her husband. She does *suiboku*," she says, referring to traditional Japanese ink drawings.

"You know, I was talking to my sister the other day and we were saying how poor we used to be. But now that I look back on it, we weren't poor at all. We had everything we needed. So many people back then suffered privations. I look back on it now and I feel we were blessed."

Goro and Katsue

On my walk back to the port I see an elderly couple sitting on a low section of the seawall. This is not the first time I've seen this tiny man wearing pants too big for his skinny frame and his rounder wife, who is sitting next to him. But the difference is that this time I know who they are.

"Hey, I just talked to your younger sister Okae," I tell the woman.

"Oh, you know Okae?"

"I never realized you were sisters," I say.

Goro butts in. "I was born in Showa 4 [1929] and my wife in Showa 6 [1931]! We walk almost every evening and stop here for a three-minute rest every time."

"Wow, so your father was born in the Meiji period then?"

"Yes, that's right. He was a fisherman."

"You're both really healthy, aren't you?" I say.

His face is triangular, and two yellow teeth stick up from the bottom gums. His tiny eyes get lost in wrinkles when he smiles.

"Nothing hurts. Not my knees, or feet. Just my brain is a bit weak," he says while pointing to his baseball cap and laughing. "I went to school here on Shiraishi, but I never went to high school. I went to the mountains in Showa 18 [1943], during the war. I worked for a big company, the third largest in Japan. There I made chemicals. Things that explode!"

His wife says, "You understand his accent, don't you, because you've lived here long enough now."

"Then a couple of years later, in Showa 20, while I was still working for the chemical company, I was on Tsushima Island between Korea and Japan when the war suddenly ended. Everything just shut down. People left their posts, didn't know what to do. There was no system in place to repatriate people or to even tell them where to go next. The army started discharging people but told them they'd have to get back to Japan on their own.

"Of course, there was no way for most people to get back. There weren't enough ships or planes and those previously in command were powerless. So no one could move. In the meantime, everything was in tatters. Many Japanese warships had been sunk, and the situation descended into chaos as bandits took over other Japanese ships. Japanese civilians were fired on and killed in the streets of China, Manchuria and other territories when the surrender was announced.

"There were Korean and American ships around Tsushima, but none of them were going to help Japanese soldiers. I was lucky because

I got home on a civilian ship. But even so, we escaped quietly under the cover of night like stowaways, hoping no one would come after us.

"We've been back on the island for thirty years now, living off our pension. If you work at a company for forty years, you'll have enough money from the pension to get by."

Goro's cap has slipped to the side making him look, uncannily, like a high school student. He starts deriding his wife. "I worked hard for forty years but she didn't do a thing! She just used all my money!"

"I just spent money and had fun. Our kids all went to university and are working in Tokyo now."

"Okae told me you do suiboku."

"I started learning after we moved back to Shiraishi, when I was seventy-two years old. I used to go to Kasaoka to take lessons. I went for twenty years but I never became very good."

"That's because she's dumb!" Goro says with jocularity.

His wife remains demure. "For twenty years I've had my art displayed in the Kasaoka Art Exhibition," she continues. "Everyone said I shouldn't quit but I'm ninety-two you know."

"Suiboku is water and ink. She made scrolls for big companies," says Goro.

"I only did about ten of them professionally."

When I asked about their marriage, Goro said, "We were married in Showa 30 [1955]. I was twenty-six and she was twenty-four. Well, this is the countryside, so of course my parents found me a wife. I was working off the island but I used to come back at Obon. You know the Shiraishi Bon Dance, right? I met my wife there. I asked her to dance. The Shiraishi dance is famous. A very nice dance."

"But he's terrible at the Shiraishi dance! Can't dance a lick!" she says, now ribbing him. By now, we're all laughing so hard we're almost rolling into the port.

"You both look so happy," I remark.

"Yes, we're really happy," he says. "We have enough to eat. Between the two of us we have 300,000 yen per month from our pension. When we came back, we immediately fixed up the *honke* [main family] house. The best things in life are your pension, food and exercise!"

I apologize for having taken up much more than the three minutes they usually allow themselves to rest. They stand up, calling out farewells as they leave. As they both walk away, I can't help notice how excellent their posture is.

A Quarryman

IT'S JUST BEFORE NOON, and I'm on my scooter headed to the back of the island. A kite soars above me as I crest the first large hill, the shadow of its wingspan running on the pavement just in front of my tire. By the time I approach the second hill, the kite has turned off towards Kitagi Island across the channel, and I have arrived at my destination. This is the neighborhood of *shimo-ura* (lit., the further reaches of the back), the domain of the rock quarriers.

The Stone Quarry

Skinny as the trunk of a pencil pine, Mr. Umakoshi wears one-piece work overalls that elongate the profile of his body to that of a soft spindled thread. He, his wife and I are sitting at their outdoor table crafted from a handsome stone slab, one foot (30 cm) thick. Hemmed in by the water's edge in the front, their modest house is protected by gargantuan hunks of granite standing on end, wedged to form a barrier between the house and the fury of typhoons. In front of the house, where the deep belly of the sea vomits up storm waves during foul weather, is a concrete edge that, in the past, transport ships lumbered up to for loading. The ship would be lined up broadside, flush with the concrete wall to wait for cargo.

"My company put in the stone monument at the port introducing the Shiraishi Bon Dance. We also made the rock with the Buddha footprints at the entrance to the Bussharito. We were the leading stone-quarrying company at the time, did projects in Osaka and Kobe, some with contracts of three to five years. We were commissioned to do rock work at the World Expo Park in 1970.

"My parents and grandparents were stone quarriers too. I'm the seventh generation. Our family started mining in Shikoku, so we're outsiders. My parents moved to Kitagi Island and quarried there, then started here about sixty years ago. We had quarries on both Kitagi and Shiraishi for a while."

Mr. Umakoshi and his wife both grew up on Kitagi in the 1950s and 60s. "Mama-san from the Nakanishiya inn lived in the same neighborhood as me on Kitagi," Mrs. Umakoshi says in a soft bright voice. "Fumi, her daughter-in-law, lived over on the opposite side of the island."

Mr. Umakoshi married his high-school sweetheart and they decided to move to Shiraishi so he could take over the quarry from his father. Their "love marriage" (so called if it isn't *omiai*, or arranged) still endures in the private glances and smiles of assurance that pass between them.

Mrs. Umakoshi brushes off my suggestion that it may have been tough being an outsider on Shiraishi Island. "We're outsiders but we're all islanders, so it's pretty much the same." They talk fondly of their two sons, one in Yamaguchi Prefecture, the other in Hiroshima, and the four grandchildren who come back to visit during the holidays. "The weather is perfect when they come during spring or summer. We go fishing, just enjoy the outdoors," the rock-quarrying grandfather says.

"We moved to Shiraishi because the rock is far superior here. Even though right now we're only 500 meters [a third of a mile] across the sea from Kitagi, the rock is different," he says. The color of the stone is different too, imbued with a hue of pink.

"We used to have eight houses next to ours doing stonework. Now there are only two, including Kio-chan's. He was our neighbor for a long time. His wife still lives in the house next door."

Long before Umakoshi was born, his predecessors spent long hours every day swinging sledgehammers onto iron pegs while their teams of sweat-dripping cohorts sang a stone miner's song to keep rhythm. *Fundoshi* cloths were wrapped around their groins. Their muscles, lacquered with sweat, glimmered in the sun while rivulets of liquid salt poured down onto the rock. Standing in a line across the apex of the slab, they pounded the row of pegs down, down,

down into the stone, each blow forcing the peg a little deeper, until *crack*—the slab finally split along the peg line. In those days even bedrock was quarried by hand and moved from mountain to sea port via manpower and horses.

"In the beginning, they used to climb up the mountain to the big rocks sitting on top and chisel them apart until they fell. Then they'd pick up the pieces wherever they landed. Have you been up on top of Pigeon Rock?" he asks, referring to a boulder on the mountain that can be climbed to gain views of the Seto Inland Sea.

I nod.

"The footholds in that boulder were carved out by hand. Sections of the walls of Osaka Castle were built with Kitagi stone and those too were put together by hand, just like the pyramids in Egypt. Before machines, they also took rocks from the sea. At low tide when the large stones were exposed, they'd go down into the water, chisel them apart, then bring them back to shore in chunks. They dug into the bedrock at low tide until it had so many holes it looked like Urashima Taro's underwater sea palace."

In 1932, when machines came to the Kasaoka Islands, the rock miners' song died out as the masons now had time to relax and lubricate their newly vacationing muscles with sake. As a stone quarrier's son, Mr. Umakoshi grew up with the swagger and macho of generations of men who turned granite to gold, and who labored to build Kitagi Island into one of the richest postal codes in all of Japan.

The men had a right to be proud. A host of well-known Tokyo landmarks were made from Kitagi stone: the nineteenth-century Bank of Japan headquarters, the flagship Mitsukoshi department store, and the Meiji Seimei Life Insurance building next to the Imperial Palace are just a few of the better-known structures. Even the stone *torii* gate at Yasukuni Shrine was made from Kitagi stone.

"But the truth is," continues Mr. Umakoshi, looking me straight in the eye, "Shiraishi rock was used to build those structures too! Stone mining goes back over one hundred years here but we only had about eighteen households on Shiraishi involved in rock quarrying compared to fifty or so on Kitagi. The big transport ships went to Kitagi first to pick up stone, then stopped by here to finish off their loads," he says, motioning to the water line right in front of the house. So all the rock shipped together on the same boats was labeled Kitagi stone.

"Since the stone quarries were very successful, Kasaoka City—who owned the land—became rich. So after that, the people of Shiraishi thought it wasn't fair that the city was making so much money from our labors, when we were only getting a small percentage of the profits. So during the Meiji period, in 1902, the temple priest petitioned to have the ownership of the mountains transferred from Kasaoka to the island people. It took many years, but the Buddhist Priest's grandfather, Shunjo Norimi, worked doggedly on behalf of the quarrymen and finally secured the purchase. After that, the mountain on Shiraishi was divided up among the stone-quarrying families and rights were granted so each family had their own quarry to dig from. Kio-chan's father had one, and we got one too.

"After we bought the mountain from the city, we had to pay it off little by little. We paid about 10 percent of the profits back to Kasaoka City and another percentage to Shiraishi Island. With this money we have, over the years, installed street lights, purchased computers for the community center, and even bought a grand piano for the school. The quarry families also foot the bill for the island sports festival every year. From that money all the food and activities are paid for. Even though there are only two houses back here still quarrying, we still pay a portion of our proceeds to the island. It's not that much anymore, but still.

"There's a monument up at the temple," he says, referring to a conspicuous plinth with a polished stone ball on top of it that stands next to the temple gate. "In May every year, before the island sports festival, we go up to the monument and pray. Engraved on the side of that stone is the story of the stone miners of Shiraishi. That's our history.

"We had transport ships coming up to the pier in front of the house until about forty years ago, when they put in the ring road. Once we had a road, trucks could transport the rock from the back of the island to the port and onto the ferry to the mainland, so we hardly ever use the transport ships anymore. We did have one come up here last year, but it's unusual these days. Most rock leaves the island by truck.

"Once the road was built, things were much easier. Relying on large transport ships meant that if the weather turned or a typhoon was coming, the boats couldn't leave Osaka to come all the way here. With trucks, we can run in most weather, up to the last moment on the island before the ferry shuts down, and again on the highways on the mainland until the typhoon hits. And now all the rock that leaves the island is labeled Shiraishi rock."

He and his wife talk about the days of yore, when everyone was flush with money. "If it even looked like rain, we'd say, 'Screw work, let's go fishing'! We'd dive into the water and collect shellfish or take the boat out. Then at night when it would get cold, we'd have a fire on the edge by the water over there and drink sake. Sometimes we'd drink all day. And we could still make a living! Ah, those were the days!" Mr. Umakoshi says shaking his head.

Stone was previously used for the foundations of houses which helped prevent termites from getting into the building. Concrete foundations absorb moisture which attracts these white ants. Now they make foundations with poured concrete. Previously, rock was employed for everyday tools too, such as milling stones and mortars for pounding *mochi* rice, all archaic now. Since tools have been replaced by machines, and structures like stone buildings and walls all use cheaper, imported rock from China, the industry here collapsed.

"Did you do any of the work on the new Shiraishi Beach?" I ask, referring to the ten-year project to lay new sand to make the beach wider. For years I've been watching this development, from the excavating and filling in of the smaller natural beach to the laying of a large apron of stones that fit together exactly, like pieces of a jigsaw puzzle. On top of that apron, sand is poured from barges.

"Nope, all the stone came from China. We asked them to use our stone because we have perfectly usable ingredients right here on the island. But even the rock that decorates Kasaoka City Hall on the mainland isn't from Kasaoka. Recently, the city gained National Heritage status for our long history of stone quarrying, but most of the rock used in Kasaoka comes from China. How do you explain that?

"Even when we get work these days, we often can't fill the orders because we don't have enough people working in stone anymore. Say the city puts in an order for a park. They always want it done as soon as possible. With just one or two houses working the quarries, there's no way we can work that fast. So we have to turn down the contract."

❀ ❀ ❀

I hop back on my steed and pass Turtle Rock on my way along the coastline. It's low tide, the only time you can see the stone's animal likeness with its carapace and head peeking up out of the water. The sun is sinking toward the west-southwest and from now on it will set a little further to the south each day. The autumn winds gently nudging the side of my scooter will soon become stronger and more persistent. In fact, when I get back to my house, white caps are already forming inside the port.

As I'm getting off my scooter, a car drives up and the driver rolls down the window. I rush to the vehicle when I recognize Mama-san's daughter at the wheel. I had recently heard that Mama-san had moved into a residential facility in Kasaoka and I'm anxious to hear what happened.

"Is Mama-san okay?"

"Oh yes, she's fine," her daughter assures me. "We brought her back to the island today to move some of her belongings to Kasaoka. She's at her house right now if you want to see her."

Of course I do.

When I arrive at Mama-san's house on the beach, she's looking just as fresh and energetic as always. Her hair is tied back in an elegant chignon. But this time she's wearing Western clothes. She sits on a cushion on the floor and explains to me how, one day, she toppled over while in her vegetable garden and cut up her face on some bushes. Her children took her into the hospital on the mainland and at that time they decided she should go into a facility for the elderly. She's been away from the island two months already.

"My daughter lives very near now," she says reassuringly. Then she smiles and instructs her offspring to bring some items down from upstairs that she has set aside. After she disappears, Mama-san laments to me that her precious silk kimonos have already been disposed of. "I told them not to touch a thing, but I can't find those kimonos anywhere."

The daughter returns, kneels and presents me with seven bolts of *yukata* cloth, a gesture which makes me feel vaguely like royalty since bolts of fabric were presented as tribute to rulers in ancient Japan. "And the other?" murmurs the matriarch. The girl trots back up the steep stairs. This time, the bag is much larger causing her to descend the steps slowly, sideways. Mama-san insists I take both. I look inside the larger sack and see one kimono and one hakama: the Shigin Odori costumes.

The Tombstone Maker's Wife

WHEN I CALLED eighty-five-year-old Amagiso to ask her for an interview, she said, "Well, I can't remember much anymore. I can hardly even remember where I put things these days."

"I just want to ask some basic things, like how long you've been running your inn."

"Oh, a long time," she says. "I open the inn only in the summertime now. It's named after Amagi Mountain behind us. There's a Hachiman shrine up there that the Otafuku inn used to take care of. They held a ceremony twice a year, so we'd attend and take offerings to pray for happiness and prosperity."

"Um, can I come over right now?"

When I arrive at the Amagiso *ryokan* inn, by far the nicest accommodation on the island, I am greeted by the doyenne herself, petite and stylish. The entryway is grand and includes a shelf for her stunning ikebana flower arrangements.

I slip out of my shoes into cozy cloth slippers and trail behind Amagiso as she glides past a Japanese Imari porcelain floor-vase next to a picture window that faces onto a completely landscaped miniature Japanese garden. Behind the glass, a tall five-tiered stone pagoda stands next to a plum tree; decorative rocks indicate mountains. Large koi carp laze about a small pond. Amagiso once told me that whenever one of these grandiose goldfish die, she buries it in her garden and prays for its soul.

She leads me into a sixteen-tatami-mat room with an alcove graced with a *suiboku* ink-painted scroll and another of her ikebana arrangements. A flower-patterned scarf knotted gracefully around her neck, Amagiso looks like she would fit perfectly in the alcove herself. I notice a photo album lying on the table.

"I was a second wife," she says through thick, ruby lips. "I'm from Konoshima. A woman there had a cousin on Shiraishi who was looking for a wife. She said his previous wife had died and he needed a new one.

"I was selling fish at the port of Konoshima Island and that lady showed me a photo of the man and his three-year-old boy. I thought the man looked nice and the kid was cute too. But the man's mother, well, she seemed a bit strict. So, I turned him down for marriage.

"Well, it turned out that the man had very good calligraphy writing skills. My mother did too. So while I thought I had cut off any possibility of communication with him, he and my mother were writing letters back and forth! The man wrote that he needed a wife as soon as possible because he had a child to care for. He and my mother had already decided on the match, so I had to stay out of it. You see, I was one of seven children. We were poor, so I had to marry him.

"I was given the child in May, while I was still selling fish at the port on Konoshima, so I'd bring him to work every day. Everyone remarked how dark this island child was, from playing out in the sun all the time.

"It's been fifty-four years since I came to Shiraishi and I have three children now. When I came, there were just under two thousand people living here. I was so busy as a young wife that I didn't know what else was happening around the island. And since I wasn't from here, it's not like I had a lot of friends or classmates to hang out with. Everyone on Shiraishi seemed to be relatives.

"Which reminds me, when I came, there were many mutes here, even brothers and sisters. You see, most of the men married other women from Shiraishi, mainly cousins, so there was a lot of inbreeding. Those people have all passed on though. Nowadays wives come from other places.

"On the far end of the beach here, we were cut off from the rest of the island because there was no ring road then. The kids took a path through the mountain to get to school. The only way to get here was to walk on a dirt footpath behind the campground, which came out over there onto the beach." She looks out the window as she talks, thinking deeply, remembering fondly.

"The sand was so beautiful then! And the sea exquisite. You could hear the waves right out front. There used to be so many *asari* clams too. Even twenty years ago people would dig for clams on the beach, remember that?"

I do.

"Then when the steel factory went up, the water turned dirty. And when they made the new beach there were no more clams.

"But our family's main business was stonecutting. We shaped and cut granite to make tombstones. There were lots of ships transporting stone at that time. From here they'd take the end products to a wholesaler in Mie Prefecture. Right out front here is where they lifted the stones onto the boat," she says, focusing her gaze on what used to be sea but is now concrete.

"There used to be so much activity around here. There were seaweed shacks all along the beach and the seaweed farmers would attach seeds to their nets and chatter all night long.

"People really worked hard in those days and many died young because of the hard manual labor. My husband was *chonan*, the oldest of seven children, so his position meant he had a lot of responsibility. He'd work late every night, sometimes until three in the morning, pounding those iron pegs into the rock. The youngest brother would wake up at ten o'clock in the morning, amble out and help just a little bit.

"Nowadays they have efficient machines but at that time they did everything by hand and breathed all that rock dust into their lungs. They used fans to keep the rock warehouses cool, so by the end of the day my husband would be completely covered in white dust.

"In those days we lived on daikon radish, greens, tofu and soup, and had to feed ten employees for lunch. Now, it's hard to believe we lived like that. Those were difficult times.

"There were twenty-two houses on Shiraishi in the stone business when I came. Then Japan started importing cheaper stone from China. We couldn't compete, so we sold all our machines for cutting gravestones. Now there are just two stone-quarry companies left on the island and I run the inn by myself."

Extravagant Funerals

"My husband died twenty-four years ago when he was sixty-six. We gave him a traditional funeral here at the house. Over three hundred people attended, way more than I ever thought would come! Seventy stayed for the meal after. I had to give a return gift to each of them so I gave out three hundred portions of sugar and boxes of detergent as thank-you gifts."

Three Shingon priests, robed in purple to indicate their highest rank, presided over the ceremony. "Our family members wore white formal *kamishimo*," she says, referring to the former samurai outfit consisting of *hakama* formal trousers and a vest that employed whale bone to stiffen the shoulders into "wings."

"All white! You don't see that anymore." She carefully slides the photo album in front of me and allows me to gawk in silence.

The first photo shows a table draped in white and emblazoned with the family crest. On top of the table is a large picture of the deceased, and a white *ihai* spirit tablet in front of it. Two black lacquer incense boxes on either side are used for the funeral ceremony when attendees pinch small chipped fragments of incense wood between their fingers, hold them up to their foreheads, then deposit the fragments back into the box onto a small mound of smoldering ash. This motion is performed three times as an offering to the dead, an offering to eternity, and an offering to the Buddha, while the heavy haze of incense is meant to blur the lines between the living and the deceased.

The next snapshot shows a small tatami-mat room with pearl-white curtains. A Buddhist deity looks down from a scroll upon plain gold floor cushions set out for prayers. The casket along the wall under the scroll is draped in dull cloth. The three cushions nearest it are covered in bright red with gold brocade and are designated for priests to sit upon while reciting elegiac verse, including the Heart Sutra. Surrounding the casket are large vases of white chrysanthemums as well as lighted candles on pedestals. On a small table in front sits a large bronze prayer bowl from which the high priests will coax long mournful sounds by tapping a soft mallet against its rim.

Another photo shows a large altar where most of the ceremony is on display. On the top shelf is another photo of the deceased, underneath which tiered shelves display fresh chrysanthemums of white, yellow and purple. In front of these are electric-lit lotus blossoms, and plump Japanese paper lanterns of the sort usually put out at Obon. Tinseled tree branches represent the trees that turned white when Buddha entered Nirvana; next to these are folding fans shut tight. Large boxes tied in black and white ribbons are gift sets of food, all bearing the names of the friends and colleagues who sent them. Behind all this are three wall-hangings: the scroll on the left a mandala; the scroll in the middle showing Dainichi Nyorai, deity of illumination; and the scroll on the right showing Buddhist saint Kobo Daishi.

Those who didn't have places reserved inside the hall stood outside and the next photo shows them clasping folded fans, the type used only at formal occasions. These attendees wear black: men in black jackets, white shirts and coal-colored ties, women in dark ebony. Schoolkids are clothed in their trademark black (boys) or navy blue (girls) uniforms. A bevy of neighborhood women serve tea while others, sitting at a long table, receive envelopes of *koden* funeral money and jot names in ledgers. Along the road from the campground to the inn is a long row of *hanawa*, round paper-flower stands with the names of individuals or companies expressing their condolences.

The last photo is one taken after the home funeral and cremation but before the forty-ninth day. The white cloth over the incense table has been replaced with a richly brocaded fabric. The white spirit tablet has been replaced with a black lacquered specimen made to order, and delivered before the day the ashes are carried to the grave. The photo of the deceased on the top shelf is now accompanied by a large decorative box holding the urn, next to which is a small box containing the *nodobotoke* Adam's apple. Below this shelf, food is laid out on two lacquer tables, one for the deceased and one for the Buddha. This altar will stay on display until the forty-ninth day when the urn is taken to the cemetery.

Amagiso explains to me the order of the funeral cortege which was a bit more detailed than the one Mimiko had described when her father died. The night before the funeral, the family gathered to decide the order of the procession. This sequence was written out vertically in calligraphy, on a long scroll over 20 feet (6 meters) long enumerating the name of each person and their duty. This genteel activity necessarily took all evening to negotiate and prepare.

"If someone who was a close friend of my husband didn't get a position near his urn in the funeral cortege, that guy'd get angry. So we had a hard time deciding who had what duty."

The person leading the procession held a flag made of Japanese *washi* paper with the deceased's name written vertically in Indian ink so people would know whose funeral it was. The other individuals were assigned different items to carry: a bamboo torch, *jinko* incense (agar wood, from a tree root that turns to incense after a hundred years), a basket holding a wooden dragon head (to guard from evil), and a collection of small colored pieces of Japanese calligraphy paper that represent flower petals. In addition they carried fresh blooms, a rice bowl, and a cup for green tea for the dead.

"I couldn't believe so many people came," Amagiso reiterates, this time with a hint of pride. "That funeral cost 13,000,000 yen. But the ceremony for the forty-ninth day was less than 300,000."

Despite the fortune spent on the funeral, she doesn't seem to have any regrets, and because their company made gravestones, they could cut back on the cost somewhat. The Amagiso family tombstones are the tallest and most magnificent in the graveyard. The pillars and *gorinto* pagoda are accompanied by a black stone tablet engraved with the deity Fudomyo-o—remover of obstacles and destroyer of evil—surrounded in crimson flames. Amagiso attends to the graves meticulously, each week replacing the flowers with fresh varieties and colors, and setting out a new can of beer on the plinth as an offering to her husband.

"The cemetery was more beautiful when people visited the graves often and replaced the flowers. Now, the blossoms are left to wilt," she says plaintively, returning her gaze to the window.

"It's a bit lonely out here now but I'm used to it. I don't have to feed ten employees lunch anymore and we have a road now. And the blue sea against the green mountains is still nice."

The Go-Between

FORTY YEARS AGO, someone noticed there was just enough room at the end of the breakwater—between the previous pastureland and the port—to build two houses if they were set so close that they almost rubbed shoulders. That's how my house came to be, and nudging the eaves of my house is Kazu-chan's. Behind my two-story abode the slope of a hill rushes down at the angle of a seagull diving into the water for its morning feed. The mountain doesn't reach Kazu-chan's doorstep though. While my house nudges the mountain, Kazu-chan's sticks out like an extension of mine. No other houses were ever built on top of this breakwater as the other parts are too narrow.

This neighborhood is called "over there," (*mukai-jo*) a directional name derived from its location when viewed from the ferry terminal on the west side. "Over there," includes these two houses on top of the breakwater as well as a well-hidden cluster of homes behind it.

The houses on the east side of the port are presided over by two *kami* (divine spirits). The mountain kami is worshipped at a stone hollow in the side of the hill. In spring and autumn our neighborhood holds a ceremony to placate this mountain spirit in hopes we will not fall victim to landslides, cascading boulders or metaphysical wrath. The other kami is a deity called Myoken, who resides in a small shrine at the top of eighty-four stone steps that stretch half-way up the mountain behind my house. From my door, rising from a patch of dwarf bamboo, the steps amble skyward. A wild azalea bush with reddish-purple petals indicates the half-way point, beyond which, at the top of the stairs, is a Shinto rope stretched between two vertical pillars indicating the entrance to the sacred Myoken Shrine grounds. This Shinto *torii* gate was built in 1843 in the belief that the shrine would protect the island from infectious disease at a time when cholera plagued the country. But the original purpose of the shrine was to honor a young woman who, in a ritual called *hitobashira* (human pillar), was sacrificed during the construction of the port. Before the practice was banned at the end of the seventeenth century, such human sacrifices were offered during the construction of not just ports, but also bridges, dams, and other large-scale projects in the belief that this would please the Shinto kami, who would in turn ensure the safety of activities in and around that location.

Myoken Shrine is so significant that a Shinto priest purifies the grounds every spring. The pagan ritual, which women are prohibited from attending, is presided over by the patriarchs of the Community Shrine Association. Recently, however, as these elders have found it increasingly difficult to climb the eighty-four steps to reach the shrine, the ceremony was moved to the bottom of the steps. The ceremony now takes place just outside of my and Kazu-chan's back doors. While women are not permitted to attend the ceremony, we both confess to peeking out from curtains of our houses.

Three days before the ceremony, preparation starts as the barber, who is a member of the Community Shrine Association, constructs a bamboo torii gate over the entryway to the steps, and a handmade reed stage. He also weaves a rope, inside the braids of which he festoons purification papers in the Shinto style. On the day of the ceremony, the robed Shinto priest and elders wearing black suits gather and place offerings of fish, sake and rice onto the makeshift altar. The Shinto priest chants ancient cryptic messages for twenty minutes, then purifies the men by passing a sacred *o-nusa* branch over their bowed heads, after which a toast of sake is made to the kami, and the annual ceremony has again satisfied the Shinto spirits.

This ceremony has been held for as long as Kazu-chan can remember, long before she came to this neighborhood as a new wife.

"Can you tell me about your wedding?" I ask her one day.

"When I was married, I wore the traditional red *uchikake* wedding kimono and *tsunokakushi* hat," says Kazu-chan. "My parents and family members escorted me from my home in Okujo to this house."

Kazu-chan and her wedding entourage walked along the sea, half a mile or so. "Onlookers crowded along the roadside to watch the procession and I tossed out candy to them. We held the wedding ceremony here at the house, but the reception was held at the Na-kanishiya inn on the beach. I remember Mama-san and her husband danced the Shigin Odori!"

The first photo she presents me with is small, with faded colors and a white framed border. It shows her, the bride, in a bright red uchikake kimono with shimmering gold threads that outline a design of broad-winged cranes, stylized puffy pine trees and sprigs of flo-rals that wrap around the sleeves and trunk of the kimono. She is at the front of the procession with six family members trailing behind her. Their footwear has faded along with the colors on the bottom edge of the photo. The men wear smart, black Western-style suits and white ties.

The other pictures are black and white and show the newlyweds sitting in traditional Japanese *seiza* style, legs tucked underneath them, with a set of parents flanking them on either side. All have elaborate meals sitting on lacquer tables set before them. By now, the bride has shed her uchikake for a plum-colored kimono with large chrysanthemums and an equally vivid obi sash. Another shot shows her posing alone, head cocked to the side as glittering hair ornaments dangle down the sides of her pleasant, but unsmiling, face. Her hands clutch a folded fan. There are no photos of the groom. As I peruse the specimens, my neighbor talks on as if the event had taken place just yesterday

"I was introduced to Takeshi through a friend of my parents. So I met him a couple times, but I was only nineteen and didn't want to get married yet so I put a stop to the relationship. Then in another year or two, the go-between came again and said to me 'Please de-cide!' I had already decided, but she didn't like my decision. But then I thought about it more and said okay. I was twenty-two and Takeshi was twenty-five when we married.

"Actually, I had considered marrying someone else who was working at the steel factory on the mainland, but my parents were against it because he was from Sendai and was planning to move back to eastern Japan after finishing his contract here. If I had married him, I would have had to go live in Sendai. It was far away, so my parents didn't want that. Now that I think back on it, I'm glad I decided to marry Takeshi."

Betrothal Gifts

"When I became engaged, my husband only gave 200,000 yen in betrothal money, about how much you'd pay for a pedigree cat these days! Twenty years ago when my daughters got engaged, the girls received extravagant betrothal gifts from their fiancés. My eldest received two million yen, a diamond ring and a necklace. My younger daughter's engagement wasn't as much, one million yen, but it was still pretty fancy."

She shows me a photo of the betrothal gifts she is referring to and I suddenly realize what those "Christmas ornaments" are in one of Eiko's cardboard boxes in the shed. The photo shows a tiered shelf set up in the alcove of Kazu-chan's home where the betrothal display holds numerous sparkly decorations each about a foot (30 cm) high. On the bottom shelf are four large square envelopes colored purple and gold: one for the diamond ring, one for the diamond necklace, and the other two for cash.

I bring in the box from the shed and ask Kazu-chan to go through it with me: a pine tree, a bamboo plant and a plum tree in bloom, similar to those in the photo, represent the auspicious combination known as *shochikubai* (pine, bamboo, plum). Two other propitious figures are a turtle and crane. All have been meticulously handcrafted by twisting long strands of paper into tight strings, a Japanese traditional art called *mizuhiki*. These strings are twisted so tightly they take on the consistency of wire and can thus be fashioned into various shapes.

Before being formed into configurations, however, the strings are painted different colors. For betrothal gifts, gold is dominant, along with silver. Green is used for pine needles, for example, but gold for the miniature pine cones on the branches. To make a cluster of bamboo stalks, the strings are lined up by color: dark green, turquoise,

lime green, yellow and gold, and bound at the end. Pink, white and red lengths are combined and curled into plum blossom pistils, stamens and petals. The turtle and crane are braided with gold, silver and green. Also in the box are several small wooden daises (on top of which gift envelopes may be laid), a piece of red felt decorated with a golden phoenix to display draped over the shelf, and a blue satin sash bearing the congratulatory word *kotobuki*.

My only question now is why is this set of betrothal gifts in the shed?

"This doesn't look like a complete set," Kazu-chan says, inspecting Eiko's box of ornaments. "So I think this must be the return gift the bride's family customarily sends to the fiancé's family. So it's probably what Eiko received after her son's engagement.

"I recently found my daughters' betrothal gifts in the storage room. I'm wondering what to do with them. There's just no room to store all this stuff. Maybe I'll take them to the next Bussharito *goma* fire ceremony."

Married Life

"Takeshi was *chonan*, the eldest of five brothers. I knew when I married that I would have to take care of his parents their whole lives, but

I had no misgivings. Takeshi's youngest brother went to college, so even after I had moved into the house, he was still coming home on university breaks, so I took care of him too. There are many stories of mothers-in-law who bully their daughters-in-law, but my mother-in-law and I are famous on the island for never having had an argument.

"My son always talks about how elegant my mother-in-law was, and he was right. Even when she died, she was perfectly poised, lying on the bed with her hands folded over her chest.

"I think she had a difficult childhood though. Her parents sent her away when she was young, to a family in Kyoto. At some point, the Kyoto family decided they didn't want her anymore, and sent her back here. I'm not sure why her parents sent her away when they only had three children. Her father was a politician, so they would have had enough money to keep her. My mother-in-law said the family in Kyoto treated her like a housemaid, so she was glad to come home.

"But because her father was a politician, she hated election times. At that time, politicians had a lot of enemies so people were always after him. That's why we have iron bars over the windows of our house. He never knew when someone might try to break in. He had nightmares about it, as if he was a gang boss! He also kept a spear hanging over the door, so whenever someone knocked, he'd be ready. In those days they had more reason to be scared. It's hard to believe now, but they used to count the election ballots out of sight, inside a van. Lots of money was flying around and exchanging hands. Gifts as well."

The Go-Between

"I've been a go-between twice. Once was for the boy we adopted into our family via *fude no oya*—when the child doesn't live with you but you take care of them. By then weddings had moved to the mainland and were taking place in hotel ballrooms. But the go-between has an important role to play in Japanese weddings even today, which is why their names are embossed next to the betrothed on the wedding invitations. They usually give a speech at the celebration. You pay them some amount of money for their time, although in my case I only received 20,000 to 30,000 yen. Professional go-betweens make much more because it's a business for them. Often the go-between is just someone who is either in a high position or one who knows a lot of people and can thus recommend a good match. But on the island, marriages were arranged by parents and their friends, or by the *fude no oya* parents."

One reason the go-between is still relevant, even though most young people choose their own partners, is that the job doesn't end after the wedding. Even after marriage, the go-between takes on the role of mediator. If the couple have problems in their relationship, they have someone to consult or, at the very least, someone to go to for support. The go-between remains impartial and wants the relationship to succeed. "But if the marriage partners have irreconcilable differences and divorce," says Kazu-chan, "they understand that too.

"It's also the go-between's job to facilitate the exchange of betrothal gifts at the engagement, so in my eldest daughter's case, although she met her fiancé at work, the go-between from the groom's side came all the way from Himeji to bring the betrothal gifts to our house. We kept them on display in the alcove until just before the wedding ceremony.

"I don't think there was such pomp and circumstance in the prewar days. Back then, people didn't have much money and I've heard that if a man was interested in a woman, he could just go empty the latrine at her house and carry the night soil to the family's garden, and they were considered married!"

Unfaithful Husbands

"You know, a lot of men used to have another woman on the side, and some had several. One guy was famous on Shiraishi for spending more time at his paramour's house than his own. The only time he'd come home was for dinner! If you didn't know better, you'd think he was the husband of the other woman. On this small island, everyone knows everything, and you can't go somewhere else to have an affair, so he became well known. I think his wife had a really hard time.

"In those days, women didn't say anything. They just put up with it. I know you hear about some women getting divorced back then, but those were exceptions. Unless a woman had money, it was difficult for her to leave her husband. Nowadays the tables have turned and women are stronger than men when it comes to the household. If a man has another woman on the side, his wife will throw him out of the house!

"Another thing that happened was a result of so many war widows. As soon as it was rumored that a woman's husband had died in the war, men on the island would start visiting the widow's house with certain intentions, and the women welcomed them. So a lot of these women would get pregnant and have children. At that time there were so many children that looked like other people's husbands! You could almost pair their facial features up with the real fathers."

Before Kazu-chan leaves my house, I open a manila envelope I'd found in one of Eiko's boxes. I show her a wedding photo placed in a cardboard frame that opens like a book, interleaved with a gauze overlay. Unfortunately, there is no name or date on it. In the lower corner of the cardboard frame is an embossed turtle, in the top corner, a crane. The picture is black and white and shows the groom in a black suit and the bride in a white wedding dress. There are two copies of the same photo, both in separate cardboard frames.

Kazu-chan doesn't recognize the people in the photo.

"Why would you give someone two identical photographs?"

"Couples sometimes give out a pair of photos to family or the go-between," says Kazu-chan.

"Could Eiko have been a go-between for this couple?"

"I don't think so. A single person, or someone divorced, cannot be a go-between. They have to be married."

A War Widow's Daughter

THE WEATHER IS COOLING, and the trees are shedding their leaves day by day, gradually exposing the smooth, round, milky-white stupa of the Bussharito. A thick carpet of fragile Japanese maple leaves line the pathway, their red and green tendrils dried and curled like little hands. The sound of clashing cymbals lures me onward. Next to the entrance is Umakoshi's rock inlaid with the footprints of Buddha. Just to the side of that is a small soldiers' graveyard.

It's November 15, the day when priests from across the prefecture come to pay reverence at the annual Bussharito ceremony. Eight priests in sartorial splendor of orange and purple silk inch slowly up the path, single file, their sacerdotal frocks swishing to the rhythm of hand bells struck to synchronize each wooden-clogged step. The line of priests ascends the staircase, enters the stupa and disappears, like the end of a rope feeding into its reel.

The bellflower-shaped reliquary has two floors. The second floor is accessed by steps from the outside where prayers are offered by the public who stand behind a barrier separated from the priests and the liturgical objects. Here, the clergy will spend the next half-hour reciting extracts from sacred books, chanting the Heart Sutra and clashing together cymbals. The half-submerged bottom floor is accessed from a door at the back of the building. Near this door, but still outside, is a tiered shelf of tombstones which stand conspicuously, shoulder to shoulder, in rows. Some have the peaked apex indicating a soldier's gravestone, others are in the shape of Jizo statues, but the majority are simple monoliths. Some are polished stone, but most are not. All have name inscriptions of some sort yet none stands over a grave. In their neat line, almost like humans standing to attention, they seem to be waiting for someone, or something. People pass by them without a glance. In short, they are treated as if they are just pieces of stone.

In a graveyard such stones replace living people: they are cared for, washed, decorated with flora, afforded goblets of water, enveloped in the aroma of incense. But these stones have been decoupled and tossed aside.

Once inside the crypt, it is dark and cool, another world. The curved walls are lined with black metal boxes decorated with family crests. The light is dim, making everything inside the room look coated in gold dust. Most of the boxes are closed, but the few that are open emanate light. Each chamber has a special key, which opens the louvered doors like wings. Inside each small nave, miniature white candles are left to burn, incense smolders in wraiths of smoke, and prayer beads are lifted, caressed, whispered to and laid back to rest inside. The doors are left open even after the relatives have left, as if to allow the person's light to shine just a little while longer.

In the middle of the hall is a tower lined with lacquered *ihai*, the wooden tablets that are representations of a person's soul. Many have gilt edges and are small objects of worship themselves. Attached to a base, they stand illustriously on top of shelves in the Buddhist altar inside the home, or as in this case, inside a sacred place because their home altar is no longer available. With the passage of time, houses get torn down, people move away and, lately, the last of the relatives to take care of the home altar passes on themselves. Who can keep the ihai of so many generations inside their own home? And who, these days, is willing to stay home to lay out the daily offerings of rice and green tea in the mornings, light candles in the memory of the deceased and swaddle them in the magical embrace of incense?

I leave the mausoleum and walk back outside, past the abandoned gravestones and over to the small soldiers' graveyard. Some of these graves are so old, they are unpolished and you can no longer read their epitaphs. This graveyard is only a small gathering of the 120 war dead on the island.

I approach a woman standing in front of a tomb. She squats down, setting out water and greens on the plinth. After a polite greeting and a nod, she says "This is my father's tomb. He went to war in Showa 12 [1937] and died in Showa 13 in the Chinese Incident. After that, there was the Manchurian Incident, then the Pacific War, and after that World War II. But now all those incidents are combined and called World War II. My father's name was Hanri Komiyama but his parents called him Ri-taro. You see?" she says pointing to the stone-carved lines of text, "It's written on the grave. The star on the top means he was in the army. I was born in Showa 10. I'm eighty-five years old now. I never knew my father. All I have is a photo of him holding me as a baby."

She has obviously told this story many times before, and wants to tell it again. I listen as she continues. "My mother was a war widow, so she married my father's younger brother. You see, at that time, there wasn't any compensation for those who died in the war. Later, after World War II, they came out with the war-widow's pension, but before then, my mother was left with nothing. Everyone living here was either a fisher or a full-time farmer and had their own vegetable gardens, so there weren't many jobs that paid cash money on the island. As far as food went, we were pretty self-sufficient. At my house we still had wheat and potatoes. I remember using a mechanism where I pushed a pedal with my foot that turned a stone to hull the wheat, but not everyone in Japan had food. But still, you need some money to get by. So a mother with children had no choice but to remarry, and since the younger brothers of their husbands were the most likely to be unwed, it was considered best to marry one of them, to keep the family together. Lots of women on Shiraishi did that. I have a sister who was born after me, the child of my mother and my uncle.

"Those were tough times, but I think that since I've been through all that, I can put up with almost anything now." I ask her name, and she says "Toyoko Hikino. There aren't many people around anymore who remember the war."

Just then a final clashing of cymbals leaps out of the Bussharito indicating the final coda of the ceremony. In the ensuing silence I realize I've been listening to the cymbals all along.

The Weekenders

WHEN I ARRIVE at the community center at eight thirty on Sunday morning, the rice is already percolating away with puffs of steam escaping from the sides of flat wooden boxes stacked three high over a small cauldron of boiling water.

The island's five children are present: the two junior high school students and three smaller children, the latter all siblings who have come with their father, Makoto. Two run amok while their limp-limbed baby sister hangs from the father's child harness. Among the handful of others who have shown up on this mid-December day to pound rice are the Tanos, a husband and wife from Okayama City who recently bought a traditional old house in Torinokuchi as a weekender. It was their veranda I was sitting on when Taiko wowed us with her stories of her husband's infidelity.

Mrs. Tano has been running art exhibits on Shiraishi for almost twenty years now. She and her husband, a teacher, are outsiders who have no family connections to the island. I approach the almost retired couple and ask them if they do rice-pounding in their neighborhood in Okayama.

"Oh no, we use a mochi-making machine," Mrs. Tano says. "It's very convenient."

A fleet of smocked ladies crowd around a long tabletop that is shrouded in a thin film of rice flour. Men of all ages hover around the steaming rice-box contraption. When cued, two of them in their sixties lift the square racks from the top of the stack while another pulls out the bottom rack near the steam and carries it to the waiting stone mortar.

Now that the steamed rice has been peeled from its mesh and transferred to the mortar, four men stand poised holding large wooden mallets. They begin pounding the rice, each taking his turn to bring the hammer down once to wallop the mass of sticky, soft rice kernels. They continue in this sequence around the circle. The unbreaking rhythm of thuds is ensured by shouts of *yo, dokkoi!* Each wallop advances the blob to a pastier state while a referee on the side whisks water into the mix to prevent the mass from sticking to the wooden mallet heads.

After fifteen minutes—and several changes of manpower to allow for rests—the rice is gaining the gooey consistency of mochi rice cake and, at this point, the assistant sneaks his hands into the pure white mass to turn it over between the potentially bone-crushing wallops.

As I stand next to the Tanos and chat, it occurs to me that while I have known them for many years now because of their work with the art exhibits, I never thought to ask them why they decided to buy a house here.

"Well," Mrs. Tano says, "as you know, for years we've been sponsoring artists to come for short-term stays to create art related to the history of Shiraishi. We hold the exhibits at Matsuura-tei, the old Edo-period house on the port."

As she starts to tell me the story, the weighty, glutinous glob of mochi is carried to the ladies waiting at the table who grab pieces as if it is bread dough. From these they will form rice cakes so delicate they sit in the palm of your hand like a freshly laid goose egg.

"When we first started the art exhibits, we stayed overnight at the Nakanishiya inn," Mrs. Tano explains, "but as we grew, we needed somewhere to base ourselves. We also thought it would be nice to have our own place to use year-round, and where we could still host the artists in the summertime."

The formed mochi cakes are now lined up in trays and a woman is walking around offering each spectator one of the globules. Following close behind is another lady with a bottle of sake and communal cups for *o-miki*, a toast with the Shinto gods. After all, the process of making mochi is itself an offering to the gods.

We stop our conversation to take part in the ritual.

Meanwhile, the next pallet of steamed rice is taken from the bottom of the stack on the cauldron, separated from its mesh and dumped into the mortar. The hammers come down in time to a traditional mochi-making song that the participants struggle to remember. They laugh as they grapple with both strength and memory.

"To tear down an old house in Japan can cost a huge amount of money, so we looked for someone who had plans to knock down theirs, and offered to buy the house and land from them for the same amount it would cost to remove the structure."

The two junior high school kids are now attempting to pound the rice by themselves. Bereft of even the slightest refrain of a mochi song and too shy to grunt, theirs is a quiet affair as the mallet heads gently poof into the rice pillow.

"We've put quite a bit of money into fixing up the house, and restoring it to its traditional beauty, but it's been well worth it. And now we can come anytime and enjoy the island events like the festivals, temple ceremonies or even mochi-making."

When the mochi now being pounded reaches its glutinous stage, an aproned woman appears carrying a basket of mugwort and tosses it into the mix. Gradually, the strands disappear into the glob as it is pounded, dying the rice a vivid green for *yo-mogi* rice cakes.

The green rice is transferred to the table, and the last pallet of hot steamed rice is thrown into the stone mortar. One of the elders, the Newspaper Delivery Man, takes the opportunity to teach his seven-year-old grandson how to hold the mallet. As the child taps the rice with the mallet head, the ladies distribute a special New Year holiday treat of *o-zoni*: hot vegetable broth in which a rice cake is submerged.

"Did you experience any problems moving to the island as outsiders?" I ask.

"Not at all," she says, before adding, "I think because we were here for so many years doing art first, and had opportunities to interact with the island people, it was easier to move here and be accepted. If we had come and started up a business, it might have been different."

As we dig into the flavorful o-zoni, Mrs. Tano tells me their plans for their island summer. "We like to kayak and we have a stand-up paddle board. We just brought our mountain bikes from the city too, so we can bike around anytime of year and take in the beautiful scenery."

The Stonecutter

THE STONECUTTER still uses a traditional bath that requires wood to be burned underneath its basin to heat it, the way all baths used to. Fuel, formerly pine needles and now most often wood, is loaded from the outside of the house through an iron door into a small bricked compartment that sits under the bath. A chimney juts out from the bricks to carry away the smoke.

For Masashi, at seventy years old, this is not the penurious act it might seem, but is rather a nod to past traditions. Anyone who has ever bathed in the old Japanese-style *goemonburo* iron bath heated by live coals underneath will tell you that there is nothing quite as satisfying. The round, one-person size cauldron is so hot, a piece of wood is sunk to the bottom of the bath to protect your feet from getting burnt as you squat in the water. These are the baths that Tetsumi, Danshi and Okae referred to when they told of burning pine needles to heat the bath, or when they related how islanders shared baths with neighbors who didn't have wells. During their time, goemonburo were the only kind of bath used on the island.

When I saw Masashi yesterday placing short, bright lengths of wood inside the iron door from outside, I stopped and invited him over for coffee.

Stonecutting

The next morning, we're sitting at my heated *kotatsu* table, looking out over the port where the large white ferries trundle in and out while seagulls soar gracefully overhead, occasionally plopping down in the water to bob in the ferries' wake. Masashi sits cross-legged on the tatami while I serve hot coffee and orange cake made from a batch of island mandarins a neighbor has harvested from her tree.

Masashi clears his throat before speaking. "I used to paint interior walls of traditional Japanese houses. Then when I could no longer make a living doing that—because the building methods changed—I started working in stone. I was about thirty-five years old then. The first year and a half I worked on Shiraishi, where I roughed new stone to make it easier for the designers to fashion into products.

"Then I moved to a small company on Kitagi Island where I worked for about twenty years. There were lots of stone factories on Kitagi in those days but they were small, with just three or four workers. A few places had thirty or more people. Where I worked there were five of us." He coughs gently into his hands.

"I'd take my boat to Kitagi Island every day to work. I liked to fish on the way over there and on the way back. It was a tiny boat, but I went to work rain or shine. Even if they called us in on a Sunday, we had to go. If it took until ten at night to fill the boats with stone, that's what we did. The only time I was excused from showing up was when there was a typhoon.

"My company didn't quarry the stone, we processed it. We received a lot of orders for stone pagodas. The requests usually came with a diagram of the product and the dimensions. You'd be surprised how many different kinds of pagodas there are: Osaka style, Kobe style, different shapes and sizes."

I've been in some of the stone factories on Kitagi that he's talking about. The round blades used for cutting the stone have teeth studded with diamonds to make them tough enough to cut through granite. The noise is piercing. The workers wear ear plugs, eye protection, and masks.

"We used fresh water when cutting stone. We couldn't use saltwater because it rusts the machinery [gentle cough]. In those days, they stored the water in tanks. What happens is this: as the water is sprayed on the stone when it's being cut, tiny stone particles are mixed in with it. A lot of this water splatters out from the moving blade and onto the walls of the factory. These particle-laden droplets dry and leave behind a fine dust on the walls. Day by day, little by little, the dust builds up on the walls. The excess water that wasn't sprayed onto the walls is recaptured and stored in holding tanks to be recirculated and used again. Then the already-dirty water gets sprayed out onto the wall. Well, that fine dust on the walls eventually enters the air system.

"While I was cutting the stone, I had a big fan in front of me. So when I breathed in that air, the dust particles went straight into my lungs.

"Nowadays people wear masks and the factories are clean but that wasn't the case when I was working. On Kitagi, there were many people who came down with lung disease. A specialist doctor came and tested us every year. I never showed any signs of it though.

"Eventually the company I worked for went bankrupt so I had no job. The next year when I went in for my regular lung test, they took an X-ray and told me to go to a specialist. The specialist turned out to be the same doctor who came to Kitagi once or twice a year. He told me I had pneumoconiosis, or lung disease.

"Anyway, after that I couldn't work anymore. So I've just taken it easy since then. I can do a little light work, but nothing too sustained. I'm chopping wood to heat my bath right now but I only do a little bit each day, just enough to work up a sweat, then I have to stop because I run out of breath.

"But I'm okay, because I was born in Showa 25 [1950]. I'm a tiger, and not only that, I'm *go no tora*." Go no tora only happens once every thirty-six years, when the tiger Chinese zodiac sign is paired with Saturn. "So that makes me especially strong, and I can overcome things," he says.

"Not many of my classmates are still left on the island. You know Ma-kun who goes out fishing in the mornings with Mr. Kawata? He's my classmate. When he was about twenty-three, he had an accident on the mainland. His car went off the road and rolled down an embankment into the Takahashi River. He was unconscious for more than fifty days."

I'd heard that Ma-kun had to learn basic things all over again: "This is a cup," "This is a plate," etc. He never completely recovered. Only one of Ma-kun's siblings, an older sister, still lives on the island.

Mr. Kawata is her husband. Eventually, Ma-kun's parents passed away but he still lives in the family home by himself. Part of why he is able to survive on his own is because the island is such a safe environment and people look after him. He, too, is a *go no tora*, going blithely on his way.

Ghosts

I've known the Stonecutter for a long time, but he's never been much of a talker. So I'm especially pleased by his continued soliloquizing, a result, no doubt of having a willing audience.

"One time when I was in fifth or sixth grade I went over to a friend's house to watch TV because we didn't have one then. In the evening, about seven thirty, I left to go home and suddenly, wow, this light floated right past me! It was a *hitodama* fireball, about the size of a baseball. But it wasn't round, it was oblong and had a tail. It didn't shoot past like a comet either, but went slowly, *fua-fua, fua-fua*," he says making his hands undulate in the air. "It's the phosphor emitted from the graves when the body decays that causes the light. This light attracts insects that clump around it in a ball. When I saw it I was so scared, I quickly chose a different route to go home.

"I think air fluctuations are creepy too. You know when suddenly your body gets cold? Maybe the wind blows a certain way and your body shudders? When I feel these variations it scares me, makes me think there's something in the air." He hacks for a spell before continuing.

"I've heard that the temple is a really lonely place, especially if you sleep there. The spirits are lonely because it's so quiet. If you go and make some noise, it pleases them.

"Speaking of spirits, did you know people can still get buried on the island? Permission has to be granted from the temple. The Buddhist Priest takes the paperwork to Kasaoka City Hall for you. I know because my father was buried on Tomiyama Hill almost ten years ago.

"Back in the olden days, when Japan still had the *shinoukousho* social stratification—when the population was divided according to occupation—we had gravediggers on Shiraishi. People at the bottom of the hierarchy had that job. But nowadays the family digs the tomb. When you dig a new hole, it's unsettling because you never know what you might find. Like the time we dug the cavity for my grandmother, and my grandfather's casket fell out from his grave!

"Anyway, my father was probably the last one to be buried on Shiraishi Island. We didn't plan on burying him. He was supposed to be cremated. But on the day he died, a typhoon was coming so we had to wait a couple days for the storm to pass and the winds to die down so the Kairyu Maru [emergency charter boat] could take his body to the crematorium in Kasaoka. But then a second typhoon came right behind the first! We couldn't wait any longer, so we decided to just bury him on Tomiyama Hill. I helped dig the chamber. Later when my mother died, she was cremated. But you know, when a person is cremated, you forget them easier. If someone is buried, you keep memories of that person forever."

The Stonecutter lives in the same neighborhood I do. So with all the ghost talk, the conversation shifts to *hitobashira*, and the story of the Woman in the Pillar. He hems a bit before saying, "My grandmother said that Myoken Shrine on the mountain behind your house was built to pray for Komiyama-san, the woman who was sacrificed. I'm not sure where they encased the woman, but I've heard it was down on the far side of the breakwater, at the sluice gate. Next to where the plumber lives."

※ ※ ※

The sluice gate regulates water flows between the sea and a freshwater pond on the backside of the breakwater. Every now and then, when the water in the pond fills up from rain or drainage, the sluice gate is opened to pump out the excess into the port. If the pond gets too low from lack of rain, the gate can be opened to empty water from the port into the pond.

There used to be a large old pine tree standing at this gate. Like many of the other pines on Shiraishi Island, this one most likely perished from the ravaging effects of the pine bark beetle. The pines that used to grace shoreline where I live—including the one that Danshi, as a boy, used to jump from into the sea—probably met their demise due to the rapid development of the port after World War II. The new building for the Fishermen's Union required even more land reclamation and a wider road for access. Other pines that previously populated the forest behind my house have been crowded out by stronger more virulent species of trees allowed to dominate now that islanders no longer depend on the tree's needles to heat their kitchen stoves or baths.

Some measure of forest maintenance is necessary for the conifers to thrive. Locals constantly mourn the death of the pine tree, a symbol of long life in Japan. The pine is said to live one thousand years. This particular pine tree at the sluice gate, however, was said to have additional meaning—as a memorial to the woman who was sacrificed in hitobashira. Many believe it was this exact location where the oblation was performed.

No one is really sure if the Woman in the Pillar legend is true, so the veracity of the story lies within the person who tells it well enough to lend verisimilitude. But I figure that among the believers, there might be one who has seen a ghost around the sluice gate. So I endeavor to ask the plumber who lives in the house across from where the pine tree used to stand.

The plumber has been busy since the beginning of summer building a low boundary around his property that butts up to the break-water. After a day of his regular work, he comes home and works on another section of the cement-block barrier in the cool of the evening. I often walk right by him on my way to the grocery store. Each week, for six months now, he gets closer to finishing the construction and soon my opportunity to ask him about hitobashira will be gone.

But the plumber is not a very friendly man. And this is why, only now, have I finally rallied up the courage to ask him.

As I approach the end of the breakwater, he is putting the finishing touches on his dear wall.

"What a nice wall," I call out to him.

He grunts and continues his work.

"Um, Mr. Plumber, may I ask you a question? Isn't this the place where the hitobashira took place?

He pauses to look up at me. He has big buggy eyes and large lips.

"The what?" he says, wincing.

"Hitobashira."

"What hitobashira?"

"The legend of the Woman in the Pillar."

"Who said that?" he barks.

"I've heard people say that a woman was buried in the embankment around here."

"That's all lies! Why would you believe such a silly thing?" he bellows, and returns to his wall.

I thank him, wish him luck on finishing his barricade, and swing around towards home.

❋ ❋ ❋

I keep returning to the photo of the war widows gathered in front of Yasukuni Shrine: which one is Eiko?

It's been twenty-five years since I met her that day she came back with her family to help clean out her home. She was seventy-seven then and all I remember is her sitting at the low tea table in the dark living room, talking with that friend of hers with the white hair and puffy ankles. They sat on the tatami mat, Japanese style, below the portrait of the Showa emperor and empress. Poised with hands on the top of the table, their slightly hunched figures cut stark shadows against the light coming through the frosted glass panes of the windows.

Why could I not remember anything about Eiko? Her voice, her smile, or the way she must have sighed as she turned to glance at her house one last time before boarding the ferry? So much had happened, and not happened, here in this house.

The war widows in this photograph I am looking at represent a lacuna in the archives of World War II survivors. We hear about the soldiers who returned, the kamikaze pilots who didn't, the survivors of Hiroshima, Nagasaki and the Tokyo air raids. We read about POWs, the military police, the comfort women, and the pan-pan girls of the Occupation. We have heard about the Japanese women who married foreign soldiers and moved to their countries. But the war widows vanished from everyone's consciousness, and remain disembodied voices of the past. Eiko was never meant to be seen.

Few people are still around who remember Eiko. This year she would be 102 years old. But I have gleaned clues about her person. I know she was petite and pretty, that the exigencies of single-motherhood led her to work as a *nakaisan* serving visitors at an inn, that she sometimes put on a yellow kimono, or an indigo *yukata* summer kimono with pure white *sashiko* stitching. She had tiny feet—size three to be exact—and occasionally slipped them into wooden *geta* sandals. I also know she joined a group of other war widows who assiduously offered prayers at Yasukuni Shrine in faraway Tokyo, twenty-seven long years after the death of a man she had spent mere months living with.

In large group photos, photographers usually instruct the smallest people to sit in the front row. This would eliminate the three lines of widows standing on the steps. Eiko must be one of the women sitting down.

There are thirteen of them seated in the first row. Their expressions are impassive, their gazes remote. And that's when it hits me. One of them is wearing open-toed sandals with a thick horizontal band spanning the knuckle of each foot. Thin straps criss-cross from the top of the band, travel around the ankle, and meet up to buckle on the side. These shoes match exactly a pair in the bag of size three footwear in the shed.

Eiko is the fifth woman from the left in the front row. She is poised with her legs pressed together in a duchess slant to the left. Her hands rest upon a small clutch. She is the daintiest, most elegant woman in the group. Now that I know it's her, I can see the son's resemblance: the thin nose, the close-set eyes, the long face.

An Accidental Hermit

TODAY I'M UP AT KAIRYUJI TEMPLE talking to Kanta, the son of the Buddhist Priest, who moved back to the island ten years ago to help his father. He is preparing to take over the operation of the temple from his father in the spring, following a grand ceremony and an official personal name change to reflect his new status. As we sit in the vast Buddhist hall inside the temple, a minuscule kerosene heater is doing its best to comfort us. The priestly traditional summer *samue* cotton clothes have been replaced by non-traditional winter get-up: a Northface down jacket and knit hat.

The temple complex encompasses three distinct areas: the Okunoin; the main temple; and the Bussharito. The Okunoin, recently designated a National Heritage Site, is where the Buddhist saint Kobo Daishi performed ascetics under a large, overhanging rock in the year 806. "In the Edo period [1603–1868], the daimyo lord of Fuuyama Castle established the Okunoin to commemorate Kobo Daishi's visit," explains Kanta.

"This temple was formerly called Jiganji, but the daimyo changed the name to Kairyuji and designated it a place for liturgy for the Heike and Genji warriors who died in the Battle of Mizushima in 1182. So Kairyuji has never had a graveyard because the purpose of the temple wasn't originally for burials and funerals."

"So who performed the island burials then?" I ask.

"Those tasks were taken care of by the priest at Nikkoji, the Shingon temple on Konoshima, the island next door. But that temple was very busy and the priest couldn't always get over here. I've heard that during the Meiji era [1868–1912] our people threatened to apostatize and convert to Christianity if we didn't agree to take on the funerals, burials and memorial ceremonies. There might be some documents somewhere recording this, but I've never seen any.

"At any rate, we started doing funerals and memorial ceremonies and that's when we also started having parishioners."

Changing Times

"Not many people come around at midnight to clang the temple bell 108 times to ring in the New Year. Before, people would line up for the chance to take a swing at it. But about two or three years ago it seems people just stopped coming. Maybe young people don't come back to their hometowns for the New Year holiday anymore? Hardly any of my classmates come back. I had twenty-four kids in my grade at the old wooden school.

"We used to be so busy on January 2, because that was the day the islanders would come pray for health, longevity, protection from disasters and so on. Also, people came to receive redemptive prayers in their bad-luck years, especially women who turned thirty-three, men who turned forty-two, and anyone turning sixty. Most of the young people would come together with their classmates, since they were all turning that age in the same year. After coming to the temple, they'd head off to the Otafuku or Nakanishiya inn for a bit of a class reunion with food and lots of sake. My class was the last to do that, when I turned forty-two, ten years ago. Nowadays, if someone does come for a prayer during their bad-luck year, they come by themselves.

"When we held memorial ceremonies on the first, seventh, thirteenth, seventeenth, twenty-third and fiftieth anniversaries of a family member's death, the mourners always had lunch at one of the inns. We had fifty people at those gatherings and that was happening every week. As a priest, I was sometimes treated to two or three lunches a day. I ate so many funeral lunches that I never wanted to see one again!

"Not only did people eat, they drank a lot more sake then too. People looked forward to these observances because they'd get together with family, old friends and neighbors and drink together. It wasn't uncommon for someone to stand up and start singing the Shiraishi Bon Dance requiem, and another to get up and perform the dance! That was about fifteen years ago. Now we're lucky to have thirty people at a memorial ceremony and people bring boxed lunches from the mainland rather than going to the inns on the island, because it's cheaper.

"I know a lot of people say we should hold events at the temple, such as meditation or sutra copying, but such events would have to be held on weekends when people are free. But memorial ceremonies are usually scheduled on Saturdays and Sundays too. I'm the only full time priest. My father is eighty-eight and helps out when he can, but he can only do so much.

"In addition, so many islanders have moved to the mainland that I go there to conduct the funerals and ceremonies because it's more convenient for family from all over Japan to gather there. I get called to do functions in Fukuyama and Osaka a lot. Osaka is a three-hour drive each way. I even go to Tokyo. For Tokyo I go by bullet train but it still takes three hours to get up there, then another hour on a local train to wherever the ceremony will be held, so that's four hours each way. I can only do it all in one day because I live on the mainland. Otherwise I'd never make the last ferry back to the island."

He admits that nowadays, the temple has become more of a hermitage than a place for people to gather.

"But at least we can still make a living at this temple. Other priests take care of two or three temples in order to make a living. There's one Buddhist priest from the mainland going to both Kitagi and Manabe islands."

Soldiers' Resting Place

"Can you tell me the history of Tomiyama Hill?" I ask.

"We never had a cemetery at the temple, so people had to buy private land to bury the dead. Sections of Tomiyama Hill were owned by different people, most who cultivated the land for growing vegetables. But they slowly sold off sections of their plots to people to use for graves. So it's not an official cemetery; there is no map or caretaker.

"When my father had the Bussharito built in 1970, we allocated a place next to it to serve as a soldiers' resting place. At that time, some people moved the graves of the war dead from Tomiyama Hill to this soldiers' graveyard.

"And of course, wherever you have a cemetery, you have *hitodama*—the disembodied souls that look like fireballs. I hear there used to be some around the temple. People said if you walked around here at night, you'd see them shoot overhead back and forth between the mountains. I've heard lots of those stories.

"When I was in elementary school there was a landslide on Tomiyama Hill. At that time, I heard hitodama could be seen rising up out of that section of the hill. I've never seen one myself but I don't want to. It's too creepy. Sometimes even here at the temple by myself, I get a sudden chill and feel like there's something near me. When that happens, I stop working and leave."

The Future of the Temple

"I'm the eighteenth generation of priest here, the fifth generation from my family. My son won't become a priest, so I don't know what will happen. It's hard to get a priest from outside to come live here. There's no road up to the temple and no parking lot nearby, so it's a difficult place to work and have a family. Heck, I can't even get Wi-Fi up here! And who wants to move to a place with no hospital and a doctor who only comes twice a week?

"Those temples in the big cities charge entrance fees. They survive because of tourism. We don't have an entrance fee to our temple and there's no hope of making money through tourism.

"You know the rock quarries on the island? They used to make gravestones for people. But now most of their work is destroying the stones, or moving them to other places, because people have moved far away and can't get back to the island to tend to them."

A few times a year, usually during the summer, I witness the process of a grave removal. A truck parks in front of Mimiko's beach shack, right next to the Bonsan Michi path. From the truck, a small machine with continuous tracks is unloaded down a ramp. This knee-high motorized vehicle has a flatbed on top of it, and is made for moving small but heavy loads. The tracks allow it to climb the long, wide concrete steps up Tomiyama Hill. At the top, two workers load a gravestone onto the machine, and it backs down the hill and climbs up the ramp backward onto the truck. The truck drives the grave away, onto the ferry and onward via the highway to the deceased's next final resting place, usually near a city.

"Or they take the urn out and build a new tomb somewhere else," says Kanta. "Some people are abandoning their ancestral graves completely. You know those headstones standing in back of the Bussharito? Those are all old tombstones that have been removed from Tomiyama Hill. We don't know what to do with them, so we keep them there."

I recall the stones, serried in rows, with names on them, inscriptions on them, epitaphs for the dead. Now I understand why those stone slabs have been decoupled, and divested of their purpose. But it is no less disturbing.

"What can the Shiraishi people do to help the temple survive?" I am eager to know.

"The Shiraishi people already do enough. They help clean the temple grounds, which is the most supportive thing they can do. Temple-ground cleaning happens four times a year, and even people who have bad backs or gimpy legs come and help. I doubt there are many temples where the community gets together to clean the way they do here. It's admirable. And it's actually better than donations.

"I suppose that some day it will get to the point where no one needs my services anymore. I'll just do maintenance: paint this, fix that, cut the grass. Maybe I'll have to get a part-time job at 7-Eleven." He laughs.

"What's the most important role of a priest?"

"You know, when I think of the Edo period, one of the most interesting things about that time was the lifestyle of the townspeople. Until then, the only history we had was that of the nobility. There were stories about aristocrats, famous people, or heroes and warriors who fought in the battles, but what about the regular people? What were they doing at that time? How did they live? In the Edo period, the townspeople enjoyed kabuki, cherry blossom viewing, theater, tea. Since the culture permeated everyone's existence and everyone enjoyed those things rather than just the nobility, the culture has been preserved.

"So one of the most important things for me as a Buddhist priest is going to houses at the end of the year to pray for the ancestors, for protection of the house and for the happiness of the family. During those visits the old people talk to me. They want me to listen to their stories, so I do. And their stories are important. They are once-in-a-lifetime experiences and it's sad that people will soon forget these things."

January 15 is *tondo*, when the islanders meet at seven thirty in the morning for a ritual burning of New Year decorations, items too sacred to be put out in the garbage.

Many of these ornaments were made during the *mochi*-rice-cake-making and *shimenawa* rope-making events in December. The Newspaper Delivery Man has set up a tepee-style bamboo construction, held together with three smaller bamboo-shaft crossbeams. Between the slats, bystanders stuff their withering decorations. *Dai-dai* fruit (similar to an orange) and rice cakes—traditional accessories for the decorations—are thrown in as well.

Now is also the time to burn the many large sacred *shimenawa* ropes used at the various tutelary shrines on the island, such as Myoken Shrine above my house, or the mountain god shrine. The thick braided rope festooned with white purification papers from the main Shisha Shrine is also a candidate.

The Cargo Ship Captain arrives on his scooter and tosses a decoration onto the fire, Mi-chan bicycles over with hers, and the Go-Between walks over with her shimenawa door ornament. The uniformed Kimihira, one of the two junior high school students, stops by on his way to school. The Pufferfish Widow comes pushing a small granny cart on top of which is a paper bag of accessories. From inside her cart, she brings out an old dented stove pot without a lid and sits it on top. Many other islanders come too, all bringing paper bags full of traditional ornaments including traditional Japanese arrows and battledores.

Lastly, *kakizome*, the first traditional calligraphy of the year brushed with Indian ink on large sheets of paper, is placed on the pile, especially by those who hope to improve their calligraphy skills.

As the items inside the bamboo construction are sparked and the smoke furls up to the gods, the locals stand around and warm their hands and hearts with its heat. They chat, laugh and catch up on news of family and relatives who came back for the New Year holiday. Up on the hill, the junior high school sits as if looking down at us, its image wavering in the carbon fumes.

When most everything has been burned to embers, the Newspaper Delivery Man roots through the ashes with a set of tongs, looking for charred mochi cakes. He finds one, rescues it from the cinders, and with a gloved hand pinches off a piece of the sooty skin. Inside the black casing is pure white, gooey rice! He hands out chopsticks and people grab piping hot dollops of the glob to taste it, remarking how tummy-warming it is on this frosty January morning. The tongs go back into the embers, searching for another round candidate. This time, a dai-dai fruit is fished out, its orange skin turned obsidian black. It is also dissected, divested of its warm fleshy sections and distributed. The Newspaper Delivery Man explains to me that this will ward off colds.

"See how all the older people brought containers with them?" he continues. In addition to Katsuko's old pot, others have also brought small buckets or kitchen pans. "Long ago we used to take the pieces of burnt shimenawa rope home. We'd mix the remains with seawater and sprinkle the water around the house to protect from disease," he explains. "See? All the old people still do this. In the Meiji period [1868–1912], we did this to ward off cholera too."

The Last Two
Junior High School Students

SPRINGTIME COMES EARLY to the Seto Inland Sea. It's mid-February, and I'm walking on the last extant dirt path used by pedestrians to move from one place to another. This bamboo-forest-lined trail stretches from my neighborhood up to the school, and provides a shortcut to the long way around on the paved road. There are quite a few houses along this goat track, and no vehicle access. A couple of shanties, tucked back in the bamboo, remain somehow inhabited.

When I arrive at the school, I walk past the Japanese garden and into the building where I swap my shoes for slippers. The island's last two pupils are waiting for me inside their classroom on the second floor. The room contains two wooden desks and a bulletin board covered with photos of their class trip to an amusement park in Shikoku. In each snapshot, the two students stand next to each other at a designated photo spot, looking more like brothers in a family photo album than two unrelated boys from different parts of the island.

Although I have seen the students at island events such as the *tondo* ritual burning of New Year's decorations, and *mochi*-rice-cake-making, and have even attended their Research Presentations held every October, I've never had a conversation with either of them. I don't even know which neighborhood they live in. So I start with casual conversation to learn a little more about their backgrounds.

"I was born and raised on Shiraishi," says Kimihira. "My sister told me you taught English in the kindergarten and elementary school a long time ago."

So his sister is an ex-student of mine! I realize I know his family—they live in Torinokuchi behind the Cargo Ship Captain's house.

Kenshiro pipes up. "I moved here when I was three years old from Aichi Prefecture. My grandfather is from here and he's a fisherman. He keeps his boat right out in front of your house."

So he's Mr. Kawata's grandson! Mr. Kawata is the man who leaves in the early hours of the morning with Ma-kun to go fishing.

"Where will you go to school after the Shiraishi school closes this year?" I ask.

"I'll be going to a marine high school in Ehime to learn to captain boats," says Kimihira.

"I don't know where I'll go yet," says Kenshiro. "I'm one year younger than Kimihira, so I have another year of junior high."

I ask them how they feel about being the only two junior high school students on Shiraishi Island.

Kimihira speaks first. "When I was in elementary school, I had a lot of senior classmen but now that I'm older, there are no underclassmen."

This relationship between upper and lower classes is especially important in Japanese schools. So, while Kimihira was able to get guidance from older students when he was growing up, there are no students to hand down his knowledge or experience to.

"But it's not all bad having so few students," he adds. "We were able to do a lot more things because there are only two of us. It's pretty relaxed around here for us."

"I think it's sad that the school will close," says Kenshiro." It won't be as lively around here anymore."

"And since all the school activities will stop, like the arts festival, the sports day, and the Research Presentations, those traditions will die," adds Kimihira.

These school events have always been open to the community. Many residents attend with the sole aim of supporting the students and giving them an audience. Such interactions strengthen community ties.

"And everyone learned the Shiraishi Bon Dance in school," says Kimihira. "Without the school, the dance will probably die too."

"We've danced every year," says Kenshiro.

"I'm a little nervous about going to the mainland to school," says Kimihira. "I think it will be harder to make friends when there are so many students."

"I don't know where I'll go next, but I'm proud to be the last student at Shiraishi Junior High School!" Kenshiro declares.

Personally I'll miss the annual student Research Presentations the most. Each year, the junior high school students have to choose one aspect of island life and write a paper. Every autumn, they present their findings to the island residents. I ask if they wouldn't mind re-iterating the major points of their autumn speeches. Kenshiro begins.

"I researched the tombs from the Kofun period [300–538 AD] here on Shiraishi Island. Three are in my neighborhood including one at number sixteen of the eighty-eight shrines on the Shirai-shi pilgrimage route. Near one of the tombs, a very old sword was found, so we believe that 1,500 years ago, people—at least important people—were buried with their swords. This sword was exactly like one found in Miyama in Kasaoka, so we can deduce that this sword probably came from Kasaoka. We also found pottery shards and tools for making salt, so we think that the people living on Shiraishi in the Kofun period most likely traded in salt."

"I talked about the recent arrival of wild boars on Shiraishi," says Kimihira. "The boars can swim up to 30 kilometers [18 miles], so we believe the boars swam here from the mainland. Almost all of the Seto Inland Sea islands now have populations of wild boar. The first boars reached Shiraishi in 2014. We're using traps to try to catch them now and although we can never get rid of them all, we can at least keep the population down through trapping. One of the problems on Shiraishi is that we don't have enough people who want to get licensed to trap and kill the boars, so we can't catch so many of them either. All we can do is protect the local vegetable gardens by putting up fences so they can't get in to eat all the crops."

Kimihira is hinting at the fact that, with an overwhelmingly senescent population, it's difficult to leave the task of boar culling in the hands of the locals. Licenses and qualifications are needed that require sitting for examinations, and even if awarded, trapped animals are extremely dangerous creatures to be reckoned with.

Long a menace on the mainland, wild boars are a new phenomenon for small islands whose populations used to be large enough to discourage wild boars from settling. With a previous population of two thousand or more, the Former Postmaster and his wife delivered mail and telegrams on foot, Tetsumi's mother-in-law walked the mountain paths to sell tofu to the workers at the stone quarries on the backside of the mountain, and Amagiso's children took the footpaths to school. Groups of devout Buddhists hiked the Shiraishi pilgrimage path, wandering into the most remote and sacred corners of the island. The mountains were cultivated with sweet potatoes and radishes that necessitated people like the Ferry Captain to carry out the produce on their backs. Even twenty years ago, productive orange groves still dotted the island. Even more recently, people like Taiko, Kaoru and their eleven children were living in mountain dwellings, and Kairyuji Temple had a constant stream of parishioners journeying to the foot of the mountain for activities, prayers, and ceremonies. All this movement discouraged populations of wild boar from inhabiting the island.

The students and I chat about the seawalls constructed along beaches previously populated with fishermen, and the collapse of the stone businesses on the back of the island. Large swaths of coastline are now devoid of people. "With continued depopulation and subsequent increase in vacant houses," says Kimihira, "the wild boar population will likely grow."

I'm impressed with the insight these students possess, and how well thought out their answers are to my questions.

When I thank them for taking time out of their busy schedules to talk to me, they reply, "Oh no, we're not busy!"

They tell me they've prepared to sing their school song for me, which I am delighted to hear. The two small boys stand in the vast auditorium, their black school uniforms silhouetted against the sapphire blue sea outside the window. Their teacher starts playing the piano and the boys croon forth the Shiraishi Junior High School song:

> The mountains of Kibi are distant
> From where the Inland Sea tides meet
> Nature, our schoolhouse garden
> Brings happiness to us who gather here
> O, our own Shiraishi Junior High School!
>
> The morning sun of Demon Hill
> Blushes with the glow of hope
> There's strength in us who strive together
> Shoulder to shoulder in friendly talk
> O, our own Shiraishi Junior High School!
>
> Down the ages the sturdy sleeve of Armor Rock
> Recalls the culture that protects us
> Braving storms, unweathered
> It brings glory to us who learn here
> O, our own Shiraishi Junior High School!

Among the scent of plum blossoms, I traverse the path from the school back down to my neighborhood before deciding to pass by the grocery store to pick up a few things. To my surprise, Tetsumi is behind the counter. "What are you doing here?" I ask, in genuine surprise.

"I'm back at the store after all these years," she chirps. "We sold the inn to a local hotelier!"

"Great news! But, shouldn't you be retired?"

"Well, Keiko's husband has taken a job on the mainland and he's commuting back and forth, so now I'm helping Keiko at the store."

Just then Taiko and her friend bumble into the store in high spirits. They call out and give me a high five as they pass, something they probably picked up from American TV. Taiko announces, "Eiji just had his baby!" and she opens up her smartphone to show me a photo of her fifth son's child, her eighth grandchild.

Newspaper Delivery Man

I'VE WAITED until the end of my year-long journey around the island to interview Mr. Amano. Not only is he the busiest person here, but he's also the most knowledgeable about island affairs. Until recently, the Amanos owned the ferry depot and pontoon, in addition to being the island's sole shipping agent. The first person one would see when landing on Shiraishi was an Amano (who would take your ticket), and when leaving the island, the last person seen would be an Amano (who would sell you a ticket to go back). They recently parted from the ferry company but still run the shipping agency out the front of their house on the port. (Now the first person one sees when embarking or disembarking is either Yakutoshi, son of the Puff-erfish Widow, or Takanori, one of the second generation U-Turns.) For years Mr. Amano was the director of the community center too. He knows everyone and helps anyone. If there's a job to be done, he's on it. If no one is available to fulfill a need, he steps in. He never vacations, and hardly ever takes a day off. And that's why he is also the newspaper delivery man.

"I was born in April of Showa 20 [1945], just four months before the end of World War II, so one of the most difficult periods that people in Japan have experienced. My father fought in both China and Southeast Asia. He had a tough time: first he contracted malaria, then sepsis. They didn't think he was going to live, but he managed to pull through.

"I'm the third son of five children. My mother died when I was eighteen. One of my brothers still lives on Shiraishi in the *honke* [main family] house."

There is no mistaking an Amano brother. They all look very much alike, and their tall, thin frames cause them to stoop when talking to a Japanese person of average height. They have pleasant smiles and gentle personalities. They're so polite, it would be rude not to like them.

"My father was the head of the Fishermen's Union for a while. After he retired from fishing, he grew flowers commercially: chrysanthemums, and bulbs for flowers such as irises, tulips, and lilies. We sold stock to flower markets in Fukuyama, Hiroshima, Kobe and Osaka. There were a lot of greenhouses on the island in the 1930s. No one does that work here anymore.

"When I was young, I helped my father do fixed-net fishing. We caught a variety of fish back when I was in junior high and high school. Then, when I was twenty-eight, I was introduced to Miwako, whose family was running the island's shipping agency. Her grandfather built the house here and ran the business. When he died in the war, her father took over. But Miwako's siblings are all girls, so there was no one to inherit the business. So when we married—she was the eldest daughter—they adopted me into the family and now both me and my wife run the business.

"Mi-chan's father [Mi-chan is what most people call Miwako] built the road that goes past here and past the next three houses, all the way to the front of where the car ferry docks. It sounds strange these days, but at that time you could get a license to reclaim land. So he funded and built this part of the road."

We're talking inside the shipping agency office among mounds of storage boxes, packages, stacks of papers and all types of scales for weighing parcels. To send a package, communication takes place through a holed window like those seen at banks. The pane of glass has so many remnants of "clear tape" stuck to it from previous notices, that it has turned gooey and yellow over the decades and you can barely see the face on the other side. We're on the customer side of the glass in the waiting room, sitting on an ancient dark green vinyl bench seat along the wall. In the corner rests an ice-cream machine that will be dusted off, plugged in, and whirred to life when summer comes and beach customers mill around waiting for the return ferry to the mainland. There are assorted souvenirs one can buy after spending a day on the island, including packets of seaweed processed in the area, and a few mulberry products produced from the government-inspired attempt to revive an ancient mulberry industry here that largely failed.

Mi-chan walks in and overhears us talking. "I've lived practically my whole life here. I've never even lived in a different house on the island. "I went to Osaka when I was eighteen and thought I'd never come back here! But my parents made me come home," she says with a pout.

"Then I had an arranged marriage. At the time, I had no idea who this guy was because he was from a different neighborhood. There were lots more people living on the island back then. There were sixty kids in my class. Plus, he was four years older than me, so I didn't know him from school either."

They seem an admirable match, with Miwako holding down the fort so that her husband is free to help the increasingly needy islanders. I've seen Mr. Amano give elderly residents a ride in his van back to their homes from the port when its raining, or in wintertime, when it's dark by the time some residents come home on the last ferry. I once watched him escort a senile resident home when she couldn't find her way. Mr. Amano is on every committee, supports every islander's random passion (or at least feigns he does) and even helped the Tanos find their weekend house. Last spring, while giving a guided tour on the island's hiking course, the seventy-five-year-old bounded up one of the boulders to obtain a panoramic view of the Seto Inland Sea. And how did he get down? He jumped.

He takes stunning photos, uses the Internet with alacrity and is the glue that keeps the island from falling apart. For a lifetime of concern for others, he recently won a national award bestowed upon individuals who have made significant achievements in the area of public service. Although the quiet, shy man was too modest to tell anyone of the accolade, news traveled from the city hall on the mainland to the people working on the ferries, who told Yakutoshi at the ferry ticket office, who murmured the news to Keiko at the grocery store, who whispered it to her mother-in-law at the Otafuku, who informed all the guests at the inn, that Mr. Amano had been called on to appear at the Imperial Palace to receive an award from the emperor.

"What was the Imperial Palace like?" I ask Miwako, regarding their recent trip to Tokyo to receive her husband's Order of the Sacred Treasure.

"I was so nervous!" she said. "There were over a hundred people lined up to see the emperor. We stood on the sidelines and were told not to say anything to him as he passed. Only one person had been designated to ask a question, to which the emperor would respond. I wore a *tsukesage* [semi-formal] kimono, beige and pink."

She points to a photo on her smartphone. She and her husband are standing side by side. Her tiny feet are in white *tabi* split-toed socks and gold-strapped sandals. She is holding a cream-colored handbag. The soft bronze-pink kimono glows in the dim light, the pale diamond pattern typical of *tsukesage* kimono sweeping up from the hem, almost as an afterthought, guiding the eye to a lively obi sash with its gold cord tied in front. The man next to her is tall, his pointy black patent leather shoes sticking out from the bottom of gray pinstriped trousers. A black coat with tails is draped over his white button-down shirt. Next to a diagonally striped tie, his medal of honor is pinned to his breast pocket. They look pleasantly into the camera, careful not to show too much pride.

"I didn't have a kimono to wear so I rented one. Well, I do have kimonos but the ones I have aren't necessarily appropriate, and when we were told there would be an assistant there to help us get ready, I chose to get one in Tokyo because it was easier than carrying it back and forth."

"I wore a suit," says Mr. Amano, "but the Buddhist Priests were dressed in formal black robes and some men wore a kimono showing their family crest. When we arrived, there was a bus to take us to a waiting room. While waiting, we were given instructions, such as to bow when the emperor opens the door and enters the room."

Miwako adds, "The kimono assistant told us to stand in the first or second row, or else we wouldn't be able to see for all the people standing in front of us. So we were right up front and we could see the emperor fairly well."

Mr. Amano continues, "When he entered the room, there was absolute silence. I was about this close to the emperor," he says, showing the distance with one of his long arms, "because he stopped to talk to someone near us. As he moved down the aisle, now and then he would pause to give a greeting to someone. The whole thing took about ten minutes. Sitting in the waiting room was much longer!"

Miwako tootles off to do other things while I change the topic to the legend of the Woman in the Pillar. If anyone knows the answer to this riddle, it will be Mr. Amano.

"At the beginning of the Edo period [1603–1868], the first phase of reclaimed land was started by the village headman, who was an Amano. The second village headman was Komiyama, who built the breakwater between 1694 and 1701. The Komiyama's house is the Edo-period house we now call Matsuura-tei, next door to the shipping agency. The daimyo lords stayed in that house while waiting for the winds and tides to change on their way to see the shogun in Edo. The lords' horses were taken off the boat and kept in a building where the post office now stands. It wasn't until the end of the Edo period that the village headman changed to Yamakawa.

"The practice of *hitobashira* was definitely widespread in the Edo period. When they built ports and bridges or when they reclaimed land, they would sacrifice a young person, usually a daughter, in the hopes that it would make the structure safer."

"A daughter?" I say, surprised that someone would offer up their own offspring.

"The landowner who was responsible for the project would usually offer up his own daughter. There is a little bit of folklore about hitobashira here, but not a lot, so it's hard to know if it really happened on Shiraishi."

"I've heard that the woman may have been encased near the sluice gate," I venture.

"I don't think it would have been near the sluice gate," he says. "The reason being that the ground there is very hard. It's tough to even dig a hole around that area. The purpose of human sacrifice was to protect the structure. Since the sluice gate is already a strong area, they probably wouldn't have felt further protection was necessary there. Of the research that has been carried out on the port, and from looking at maps, it's thought most likely that such a sacrifice would have taken place on the opposite end of the breakwater, near your house."

"Really?"

"You know how the wind is so strong at your house in the autumn and winter? The winds sweeping in from the sea hit that part of the island first. Before the modern set of concrete jetties was constructed, storm waves rolled into the port and hit the area where your house is. Plus, that's the end of the breakwater, where it butts up to the mountain, so it's potentially weak because it's a join where the two parts intersect.

"Geographically, it's a harsh environment 'over there.' That's probably why people have traditionally revered the *kami* [divine spirits] so highly on the mountain behind your house. Myoken was the tutelary deity of Komiyama who built the breakwater. He constructed that shrine and the steps come right down to the back of your house, at the join. The shrine to the mountain kami is nearby too. With such deification, it's likely people felt vulnerable to storms and natural disasters and were seeking protection by putting in those shrines. So it makes sense that the Woman in the Pillar would also have been buried there."

In the pregnant pause at the end of this conversation, Mr. Amano's son, Makoto, walks into the shipping agency. He brings out a folding chair and sits down in front of me. Makoto is my last interviewee.

Stay-at-Home Dad

MAKOTO is the Amano's second son. He is the father of the island's three small children: one of elementary-school age, and two under the age of five.

"I went to university in Nagasaki. I worked for a company based in Kyushu for ten years but I was constantly being transferred, so I eventually came back because I didn't want to go to cold places like northern Japan. When I first returned I was doing medicine deliveries for the doctor here. My parents were busy selling ferry tickets and running the shipping agency, so there was plenty of work for me.

"I met my wife in Kasaoka. She's a nurse at a hospital there so commutes back and forth to work. I stay home with the kids, but I also do lots of jobs around the island such as delivering packages for the shipping agency. I do office work for the island's Community Development Committee, including their finances.

"My oldest son, Minato [which means harbor] is in first grade and takes the school boat to elementary school on Konoshima Island. At first, we were worried about him taking the ferry to school because there are times when the boats have to stop because of strong winds. What happens if our child gets stuck on Konoshima and can't get home? But when the city decided to sponsor a dedicated school boat for elementary school-age islanders, we felt a lot better about him commuting by boat since someone would be taking responsibility.

"I'm from Shiraishi, so we're used to changeable weather conditions—if there are strong winds, we just don't work. But employers on the mainland don't understand this, nor do the schools, so it's stressful for my wife and kids sometimes when they're expected to be places.

"At the time Minato was born, the Shiraishi Elementary school was still open, but he was the only small child living here. The Octopus Hunter's kids weren't born yet and the youngest child attending the elementary school was Kenshiro, who is in junior high now, so that would have been a pretty big age gap between two students. If the school stayed open just for Minato, the next child to enter the school after him would likely be from our family too, so neither of our kids would ever have any friends or classmates. So, in the end, we decided to not worry about educating the kids here on Shiraishi. Subsequently, the elementary school closed because there were no more children to attend."

The closing of both the elementary and junior high schools has another, less obvious effect. Up until now there was another category of U-Turns: single parents returning to the island with children after a divorce. Although the island has had two cases of fathers moving back with children after a divorce, usually it is newly single mothers seeking the support of their parents to help raise their children. A returning son or daughter can live either with their parents or in an empty relative's house, almost as if they had never left the island. They'll have the support of friends, family and community here. Their kids could even attend the same school they did. In short, it's a familiar and safe environment to return to.

Because the elementary school closed three years ago, and the junior high school is closing at the end of the month, moving back to the island with children is no longer an attractive option for single parents because their children will have to take the school boat to another island—something many parents don't want to risk—and all after-school activities will also take place there.

"I think the best job you can have on the island is one you can do while also raising kids," says Makoto. "My wife works on the mainland but we still worry about her not being able to get to work or back home if there are high winds or a typhoon. Just like the old days, my parents help look after my kids. But if you live on an island and don't have family to help, it's hard to live here.

"When I moved back in 2011, there were still 680 residents here. Now the population is 430, so we lose over 20 people a year. Some pass away, some move into hospitals, and some move to the mainland to live near their grown children. People also go into residential care facilities much sooner than they used to. They used to wait until they really couldn't get by on their own anymore."

This last point is a result of the retirement of the Kairyu Maru emergency charter boat that played a significant role in the community. First, it acted as a marine ambulance for health emergencies, especially those occurring in the middle of the night. One telephone call to the captain, who lived in Torinokuchi, and he'd be at the boat in a matter of minutes. He could deliver the patient to a mainland hospital with a pontoon in front of it within twenty minutes. If the illness required a special hospital, he could deliver the subject to the most convenient port on the mainland for an ambulance pick-up.

At around the same time the Kairyu Maru was retired, our elderly resident doctor passed away. He was replaced by mainland specialists who visit twice a week. With neither a full-time doctor nor an emergency services boat, many residents aren't comfortable living so far away from medical care, and therefore spend their final years in care facilities on the mainland. The trend is also on the rise to move even healthy family members, like Mama-san, into residential care facilities because it is more convenient for their mainland families to provide for them. Within two months of Mama-san's move, one of her elderly friends from the island moved into the same facility because she was too lonely here by herself.

There was one more essential service provided by the Kairyu Maru: to transport the deceased in pall-draped coffins, together with next of kin, to the mainland, where a hearse would meet them and take the family to the crematorium on top of the hill. One of the most poignant scenes of island life was when the Kairyu Maru, upon leaving Shiraishi port, let out an extended forlorn whistle to indicate that an islander was leaving for the last time.

Without the Kairyu Maru these days, the few people who die from natural causes inside their island homes are transported to the mainland via a chartered water taxi.

It has gradually become apparent to offspring—most who live in big cities—that it is far more convenient to hold all mortuary services at a dedicated funeral hall on the mainland. Thus, in a reversal of island convention, the temple priest commutes to the mainland to perform funerals nowadays, rather than conducting them on the deceased's home turf.

"What I'm worried about is what will happen to the island when people like my father—the septuagenarians—grow too old to do things anymore. These people do so much for the island. But who will replace them?"

I ask Makoto how he thinks the island will evolve in the future.

"Well, the population won't increase, that's for sure. But more and more people are getting tired of living in cities and are moving out to the countryside. And more people work online from home these days, so I think that trend will continue. I have friends in Tokyo who say it's really hard to raise kids there: they play mostly inside and don't get enough exercise. Appealing to these people is the only way to get more people to move here.

"Of course, we always worry about what will happen when the population decreases further, but we can't just talk about the negative things. If people only talk about how inconvenient it is to live here, then no one will want to come. My kids love it here. If people knew how fun island life can be, I think they would want to experience it."

"Do you have any ideas how to get people to consider moving to the island?"

"Well, you know all the inns on the beach that hardly do much business anymore? I think we should make shared housing out of them; let people live there. If you have a beautiful place to live that is affordable, people will come. Even the school could be converted into living space. It's a nice building with a gymnasium and all. We have to think about these things.

"We can't solely focus on the elderly. Young people are also important. We need both. The people who have the most fun here are the U-Turns, like Takanori and Shinobu. They live the ideal island life. If we have more people like that, the island will do very well in the future."

At the end of February, Panken, the son of the family who used to own the bread shop, blows into my house like a gust of wind. Most islanders don't knock on doors or ring doorbells; they just walk in and call out.

For years Panken has been taking care of his elderly mother at home. I don't know him very well, but we always say hello when we pass, and we occasionally stop for a small chat. This is the first time he has ever come to my house.

He hands me a calendar for the new year and, in his voice that is always too loud, announces that his mother will be going into a care facility in Kasaoka, so he will move off the island to be closer to her.

I thank Panken for the news and ask him in what month and day he was born. I want his birthday to be the first entry in my new gift.

He misunderstands my intention and tells me there is no need to return his gift with something in-kind. The calendar was a freebie from a local business in Kasaoka, he says.

That's when I realize that the calendar, given to me at the end of February no less, was really just an excuse to come say goodbye. I thank him again for the kind gesture, and he apologizes for having interrupted me at home. Then he leaves. I haven't seen him since.

When I pass Panken's old bread shop later, I notice the electricity is still hooked up. The last several months of bills have been placed under a rock and are flapping in the wind.

From the shop, I continue walking home through the village to the port. As I make my way down the breakwater, a passenger ferry toots its horn and enters the narrow expanse between the two lobster claw jetties. But suddenly the ferry loses power, slumps to a halt, and waits, floating. Across the water Yakutoshi is standing on the pontoon, his arms forming a large cross above his head. The ferry reverses course and accelerates out of the port. There are no passengers to get on, or off.

The Foreigner

WHEN I MOVED to Shiraishi Island in 1997, there were 970 citizens in the official registry, a little less than half the population of its heyday in the 1960s and 70s.

I'll never forget my first visit to Shiraishi when I stepped off the ferry and was met by the pungent aroma of fishing nets. These bright orange membranes were heaped in dripping piles along seawalls while trawling nets were spread over the laps of cross-legged fishermen sitting on bare concrete. Hunched over like watchmakers, they mended their nets by knotting the holes back together with thread. Another fisher, his face hidden under a wide brimmed straw hat, sat reaching inside an octopus pot, a hollow scraping sound echoing from inside as he released barnacles from the walls. Toothless old ladies smiled and said "Konnichiwa" while leaning on canes and watching over the seaweed they had gathered that morning and strewn over reed mats on the road. This limey green transparent plant, after hours of sitting in the sun, would turn deep green, shrivel into thick crinkly spirals and sweat out a crusty sea salt.

These islanders lifted their gaze from their tasks to bow their head in greeting. To me they were strangers, but they knew who I was: another foreign guest come to stay at the Shiraishi International Villa, a five-room lodge perched on the apex of a modest rise with scenic views of the sea. Built in 1988, the intention was for the accommodation to provide foreign visitors the chance to encounter first-hand the lifestyle of one of Japan's 250 small inhabited islands dotting what the Japanese call the Setouchi, the Seto Inland Sea.

During this five-day sojourn at the International Villa in mid-February I witnessed a tempest blow waves over the guardrails along the road. Prompted to take shelter from the howling winds that blew sand into my face, I discovered the sunny, dead-wind zone of the interior where snowflakes pierced the frigid calm. When the weather cleared, I tramped along the ridges of the island's bony spine, marveling at all the rock formations, especially the boulders that appeared determined, at any moment, to tumble down onto the residents and wipe their village out of existence.

Before boarding the return ferry to the city, I expressed to the owners of the shipping agency my desire to rent a house in this exotic land that appealed to my survival instincts. But since Japan is a country known to be intolerant of immigrants, and where foreigners forever complain of not being accepted, I never expected to hear back. A few days later, however, a phone call came from the man at the shipping agency, the current Newspaper Deliveryman, confirming a recently vacated dwelling on the port—Eiko's house.

Although I was the first non-Japanese to live here, I believe it was my foreignness that allowed me entry into this insular community. The cloistered islanders, their curiosity piqued by the prospect of having a blond-haired, blue-eyed university teacher amongst them, considered me more of a novelty than a threat. While I was perceived as a guest from abroad who aspired to dabble in Japanese culture, the Shiraishi people also presumed that, after a year of experiencing the realities and inconveniences of island life, I would leave. Twenty-three years later, I'm still here.

Other outsiders have not been so lucky. Resistance to newcomers is so intense that prospective residents require local government approval from the mainland to move here, a process designed to filter out "undesirables" and permit only "ideal residents," the criteria of which remains undefined. This is, unfortunately, an inequitable process that systematically excludes those with a genuine interest in residing here because of some often cursory flaw.

There are ways to circumvent the admission process. Nearly half the outsiders living here have wheedled in through the back door, by requisitioning an islander to track down the owner of an empty house and request they rent it to their friend. But still the community is loathe to accept outsiders who bring their unsavory habits with them. Consider the arrogant politician who built a weekend cottage to hide his trysts from his wife and family, or the young beatnik couple with plans to live a "zero yen" lifestyle without having to work, while their flummoxed neighbors have labored their whole lives to achieve their current lifestyle. There's the quiet man who keeps to himself and dodges questions of his past, and a four-time divorcee who, despite being a promising factotum doing chores for the aged residents, turned out to be addicted to pachinko slot machines, mired in debt, and even ran a business of illegal dumping. Alcoholics, those living on the dole, and drifters of questionable morality are perceived as threats to a tight-knit community of 430 with strict social mores, whose members have known each other their entire lives and who even share the same ancestors.

If any of the above interlopers had kinsmen to smooth over relations and assume a modicum of responsibility, the hoi polloi would tolerate the occasional rogue amongst them. But when those outside familial jurisprudence bring their woes, it hardly seems fair to pile more responsibility upon villagers who are already stretching their resources to maintain harmony among a decaying community. With a local authority to screen prospective incomers, residents feel there is someone to not just take responsibility, but to right any wrongs that might be incurred.

I, too, was not an exemplary tenant when I first moved here. From the outset I upset the social milieu as I strode among the community in short shorts and a tank top, washed the windows of my house in a bikini, and invited my foreign friends to the island for all-day barbecue parties where, outside on the street, we gyrated to Latin music blasting from the stereo speakers inside. One time, in what I am sure was an island first, an exasperated neighbor flung open their top-floor window and shouted his disdain. We couldn't fathom why he was so upset. It was only nine in the evening.

Later I wed an Australian, another alien who would commit quotidian misdemeanors such as working bare-chested in his tool shed, and building a small floating platform—to aid boarding our boat—without requesting permission from the Fishermen's Union, even though there was no official requirement to ask. In a matter of

days of his arrival we had insulted the elders, and proven our igno-
rance of island customs.

As foreigners, our callowness has been forgiven, many times over,
but accepting more outsiders, whether foreign or Japanese, will require a willing change to the gestalt, a prospect that has been met with
resistance. Invariably, a divide will endure between factions willing to
tolerate change in order to thwart depopulation and those who yearn
to simply retire to the familiarity of the place they've lived all their
lives, while recalling with fondness the prosperous days gone by. In
the meantime, abandoned houses increase, the wild boar population
flourishes, and the stone deities along the pilgrimage path, further
consumed by weeds, retreat to the mountains they were carved from.

What I didn't realize when I first came was that this enclave was on
the cusp of vanishing traditions. Children still traipsed up and down
the mountains after school and glided through the cool salt water on
weekends, their lives devoid of cram schools and college entrance ex-
ams. Uninhibited, they grew up as naturally as the trees and danced
in the wind like wild flowers. Ten years ago, the last generation of
kindergarteners memorized the Bon dance for the souls of the Heike
and Genpei warriors who perished in the Inland Sea eight hundred
years ago, while junior high school students beat the *taiko* drum and
quavered to the droning dirge. All those students finished school and
moved "over there," a place that previously indicated the other side of
the port but now refers to a place much further away: the mainland.
People no longer ask if they'll come back.

Anti-cholera rituals that have been in place since the Meiji period are carried out by only the two or three who still remember the
custom passed down from their parents; one of Japan's few extant
Shinto festivals to extradite crop-destroying insects via iambic drums
rolls and the clangor of cymbals is carried out by a mere handful of
remaining practitioners; over three hundred years of prayers to the
kami (divine spirits) for the sacrifice of the village headman's daugh-

ter in the Edo period is nearly extinct, with five elders hanging on.

Nature worship has been replaced by a more practical, convenient life of industrialization, gadgets, and concrete. Shiraishi Beach, previously a small strip of natural sand that disappeared at high tide has been transformed into a wide strip of artificial granules made from crushed rock shipped in from China: a manmade fill, prone to sinkholes and crevasses when pounded by storm waves. A concrete wall was constructed to hold back surges.

The island's beach customers have changed too. Demure girls in one-piece swimsuits have been replaced by more assertive beauties sporting sculpted bikinis, ordering their boys to buy them drinks, fetch their cigarettes, or look after their small child while Mama downs tequila sunrises. Young girls—who, in more innocent times, were cajoled to join boys in their rental rowboats—now perch on the back of gleaming jet skis and scream their heads off while their testosterone-laden drivers deftly corner the high speed machine into a spin-out, the force of which hurtles the frightened belle into the water. Two years ago one of these guys fatally launched a girl into the path of an oncoming boat. Gangsters in racing boats clog the airwaves with deafening noise as they troll up and down the strip of water parallel to the beach, against the backdrop of factory smokestacks chugging out black smoke. No one likes these day-trippers, but the beach businesses put up with them in a last-ditch effort for survival in a rapidly depopulating nation that offers fewer customers each year. And while for now these delinquents are a petty weekend annoyance, imagine what would happen if just one of their kind moved here.

While inhabitants are aware they need to embrace change, acceptance can be difficult, even impossible. Even in their own protective bubble, they feel the demise of island life through aging and depopulation. Neighbors who formerly zoomed around astride bicycles, have given up the balancing act for the safer mode of walking. Those previously dedicated to evening strolls along the road, their backs straight and proud, have gradually bent over like rice heads at harvest time. I've watched my neighbors' flawless skin furrow to deep wrinkles, and I know they must be observing the same in me.

The insults of aging are numerous, and the next progression is from two legs to assistance by a third: a cane. Some then lay the stick aside to lean upon a cart and allow the wheels to entice them forward. Finally, in a last defense of independence, some willingly adopt the four-wheeled electric cart to remain mobile.

I used to be disconcerted that residents seldom ventured to the mainland to visit their previous neighbors after they went into elder care. Now I know firsthand that one small trip to those shores takes an entire day: a dedicated plan that doesn't include picking up a few necessities in town, fitting in a rendezvous at a local coffee shop, squeezing in a dental check-up, or returning a library book. Non-ve-hicled islanders are beholden to train schedules that run curtailed schedules on Wednesdays; department stores that close on Tuesdays; inopportune start times of malls and supermarkets; and vexingly early afternoon closures of banks. An additional ten-minute bus ride from the train station can dictate the difference between sharing lunch with your friend, or just a cup of tea before you must retrace your steps to make the last ferry back home at 5:00 p.m. Add the sometimes adverse climate: choppy seas, bitter cold winds, smoth-ering heat and humidity, or the drenching summer rainy season, and opportunities for the elderly to leave the island become very few.

Although I'm at least a generation younger than most living here, I've slowed down too. I no longer run through the bamboo forest, preferring to walk among zelkova, chestnut and camphor trees. Re-cently even walking long distances has become more difficult. When-ever an islander moves to a care facility, I am reminded that my own life here will also become more of a challenge, being so far removed from doctors, hospitals and mainland friends.

One day, while working on this book, the humid air hanging among the branches in the forest in back of my house suddenly popped, and time stood still for a few seconds as I breathed in the scent of newly snapped tree branches and freshly turned soil, after which an abrupt slam sent the house rattling in its stone foundation. A rock, the size of an economy car, had wedged its smooth chin firmly into the corner of the house. Luckily, the only thing in the old boulder's way was the bathroom, and no one was using it. The rock didn't budge until the quarry men arrived, busted it open with pegs and mallets, and carted its shards away in their arms, piece by chiseled piece, to the waiting bed of a pickup truck, where they whacked it further with sledgehammers until its granules were small enough to spread as fresh gravel onto the dirt parking area of the shipping agency.

Like a stubborn ancient, I'm not ready to leave this place, that somehow still appeals to my sense of adventure. I'd miss the oddly soothing sound of the docks creaking outside my window, the wind funneling through hollow masts to produce a sound like singing whales. Here, I can watch stingrays arch their expansive pectoral fins as they leap from the sea, and hear *bora* fish skip-jump across the port. I can sit on the dock at night and watch fin-propelled sardine pods churn through the water, noisy like rain on the surface of a lake. On this island, I have sat in the eye of a typhoon, seen how octopus are hunted, learned to dance under the moonlight, and wandered like the poet Basho on an ancient pilgrimage trail. I'm still content to watch lavender-colored sunsets from Shiraishi Beach in bare feet rather than from a posh restaurant atop a grand building.

Something prevents me from letting go of the past, Eiko's past, with neighbors who still live it, who spend long afternoons chatting over tea, collecting seaweed, bracken and bamboo shoots, and where I can hear the distant bell of a rotary dial telephone. A place where time is measured not in years, but by the height of a Chinese fan palm, which is now taller than my house.

Eiko

I continued to gather clues about Eiko and have arranged these distilla-
tions into the following "interview" in which I endeavor to tell her story,
and that of other war widows, as truthfully as I can.

EIKO NAKAGAWA, Taisho 9 to Heisei 15 (1920–2003)

I was born in Taisho 9 and grew up "over there" in a house behind the
breakwater. In 1944, I had an arranged marriage to Shoichi Nakagawa, the oldest of five children. When we married, Shoichi was twenty-six and I was twenty-four. It was a simple celebration, but a happy
one among the bleak rigors of life during World War II. Before the
wedding ceremony, I walked in a simple kimono from "over there"
to the house where he lived in Okujo, in the interior of the island.
After the ceremony, we had a small party with friends and neighbors.

The islanders loved to sing *hauta*, short celebratory songs. So
whenever there was a happy event, people would come around to
the house and have a bit of a tipple, which would inevitably lead to a
song. For our wedding, it was the Takasago song:

> You, my dear wife, are to live to be a hundred
> And I to be ninety-nine . . .
> Until our hair is white as snow

Just six months later, when I had fallen pregnant, Shoichi received
his draft notice for the Imperial Japanese Army. Whenever one of our
young men was called up to fight, the whole island would go to the
port to see the boys off. Even the elementary school students were
there. The new recruits made speeches with bravado. I was proud
that Shoichi was fighting for our country and I hoped he would come

back for a visit soon. He thanked his parents and his ancestors in his speech and prayed to the gods that I would deliver my baby safely in his absence.

We saw off the conscripts by waving small Japanese paper flags, and the mayor assured them that—should they not return—they would be bestowed the honor of being enshrined at Yasukuni Shrine in Tokyo.

At that time, I was living in the *honke* [main family] house with Shoichi's parents. I knew they would help me with my child. When baby Emiko was born, it was a great celebration at a time of worry and sadness. The island people came over and sang hauta around a circle, with the first person introducing a ditty and the next person leading into another song after that, following a well-worn repertoire:

> Daikoku the good god and faithful goddess
> Ebisu, god of good Luck . . .
> A newborn babe
> Is the god of blessings

Which lead into the next:

> A crane dances over our home
> It dances the dance of plenty
> And good fortune

And that lead into the oft-sung fishermen's song, "The Sea Bream's Child," about a baby fish:

> A happy birth is the sea bream's child
> Coming into the world looking like its parents
> Its face flushing faintly pink
> Its tail a paper fan
> And its eyes, above all
> Beaming ahead with good fortune forever

After Emiko turned one year old her grandparents gave her a set of Hina Dolls to celebrate Girl's Day on March 3. It was not a new set, but one handed down from her grandmother.

Emiko was a colicky baby, but a happy one. I carried her on my back when I went to collect pine needles to heat the bath and when I went to till the vegetable garden. But things took a turn for the worse when my mother-in-law suddenly caught a viral illness and died within days.

Then, in May, we heard that American planes had bombed the country at the Battle of Okinawa. It was said that the American weapons were so superior, that the Japanese soldiers didn't even try to fight back; they just ran and hid. These last months of the war were when most of our soldiers died.

I didn't know it at the time, but Shoichi had been deployed on a boat to the Philippines. It was weeks later that I found out he had gone down with his ship in the Pacific Ocean, while headed to Luzon.

The Shiraishi Island people all went to the harbor to meet the soldiers' remains when they were sent back. Some families walked carrying a framed photo of their son. When the remains arrived, the other islanders were instructed to bow and say "Congratulations" to those of us whose family member had sacrificed his life in battle to serve as His Majesty's Humble Shield. We each received a box with the remains of our husband, father or son. There was nothing inside mine. It was completely empty.

We held a mass memorial at the wooden school, all the boxes lined up to represent the soldiers, some with bones inside, many without. Some of the deceased had been fathers of schoolchildren.

Then there was Hiroshima, and the great flash of light seen from miles away. When I heard the emperor announce that Japan had surrendered, I felt neither joy nor sadness; only relief that the war was finally over.

I had only six months with Shoichi, but we had produced a beautiful daughter. That was something. I continued to live in Shoichi's house, taking care of my child and his family.

War widows in Japan had it tough. Some were discriminated

against as being wives of ghost soldiers. What would happen to me? There was no life insurance or pension available for the families that the deceased left behind.

Many of the markers on Tomiyama Hill have no remains buried there. They are just cenotaphs because no one knows what happened to these men in the war. Those family members who had kept some memento of their loved ones, such as a lock of hair, buried those items at the markers, but the bodies and bones aren't there.

There were twenty-two war widows on Shiraishi Island. Some of them married their husband's younger brothers. But I didn't want to marry Shoichi's brother. Besides, I was fine living with his parents and taking care of them along with my child.

Then plague and pestilence hit the island again. The children were the most vulnerable and several babies died from diphtheria, including baby Emiko. I tried to get help but there was little medical attention at that time, and no medicine available. Everyone suffered privations. Emiko was buried on Tomiyama Hill, and I sometimes heard her cry in the autumn wind.

With both Shoichi and Emiko gone, there was no longer a blood connection to Shoichi's family. Shoichi's younger brother, who would later be promised to Katsuko, took over the honke house. So I went back to my parents' house "over there."

By the end of the war, 101 of our island's young men had been killed in World War II combat. A nationwide movement was started by parents who lost their sons, and wives who had lost their husbands, to push the government for compensation. Finally, in 1964, the Act on Welfare of Mothers with Dependents and Widows was established and payments were dispersed.

With the establishment of the war-widow's pension, there was also a commemoration ceremony held at Shirayama Park in Kasaoka for those lost in battle. Many officials attended and laid flowers on the memorial. The widows of Shiraishi Island also attended.

But I didn't receive the war-widow's pension. Shoichi's father kept it because by then I was living with my parents again and I was no longer a relation. Shoichi had been their son for much longer than he had been my husband, so he felt he deserved it more than I did.

I worked as a *nakaisan* serving guests at a local inn to get by. Eight years later, I met a man who was working on a government project here on the island. He was staying at an inn with his colleagues. In 1953, I became pregnant. But the man could not marry me because he already had a wife and children on the mainland.

But when my son was born I felt a sense of renewal. I lived with my parents and raised him. His father helped out by sending a little money every month. I still had plenty of worries though, because in those days, people looked skeptically upon sons who were raised without fathers as role models, thinking they might not be tough enough to do a man's job. But my son had good fortune. After graduating junior high school in 1969, at fifteen years old, he obtained an apprenticeship as a boat captain.

As war widows, we were encouraged to remain faithful to our deceased husbands who gave up their lives defending our country. The Japan War-Bereaved Families Association was established for relatives of deceased war veterans, and they sponsored a trip to Yasukuni Shrine in 1974. Myself and seven other war widows from Shiraishi Island took part. That same year at Yasukuni Shrine, a memorial to Japan's war widows was completed, apparently paid for by children who had lost their fathers in war. We were able to see the bronze statue of a mother and three small children crowded around her.

In August of 1971, when Shoichi's father died, the pension was finally handed over to me, and the payments from my son's father stopped. In the meantime, my son was doing well. He captained boats to Taiwan and spent eight months in the US. He kept saving his money and ten years later built me a house on the breakwater. Shortly after that, he became engaged to a woman in Shikoku. We sent her *yuino* betrothal gifts made of twisted *mizuhiki* paper which she returned to me in kind.

I've learned not to be sentimental, but I did keep baby Emiko's Dolls Festival cart and ox and one of her kimonos. The rest of her things were burned at the temple's *goma* fire ceremony and returned to the gods.

Most of my family left Shiraishi soon after the war ended. Some went to Chiba and others to Osaka and Nagoya seeking jobs. My cousin, who also had a house on the port, left the island too. His house was next to mine, but not on the breakwater, and nearer to the Fishermen's Union. It was torn down soon after he left. He sent me photos of his daughter's wedding, and I couldn't believe how lovely she looked in a fashionable pure white Western-style bridal dress.

I've never forgotten Shoichi, which is why I always kept the photo of the Showa emperor and empress up in my house. He fought for his country. He did what was thought honorable at the time. He gave up everything for Japan.

Epilogue

THE CALL OF THE BUSH WARBLER heralds another spring, and the year-long journey around my neighborhood is coming to a close. Rosy-cheeked women turn over the friable native soil to plant vegetables, stooped men play gateball, and the sea is lapping up against the beach in soothing pulses.

I'm with the Cargo Ship Captain, sitting on beach chairs, looking out at the hazy vernal sea while watching two newly returned retirees collecting seaweed washed up on the shore. I hear they've come back after forty years in Osaka. They'll use the seaweed to fertilize the vegetable garden at the back of their house just off the beach. The robust woman is grabbing soaked clumps of knotted sea grass, heaving them onto the wheelbarrow. Her lanky husband muscles the load over the sand while the top-heavy tray tips from side to side. The couple laughs as if they are children collecting seaweed for the first time ever, when in fact, they are drawing on memories of their past, and relishing this return to childhood.

Meanwhile, Shinobu is in the midst of holding the ten-day-long Doll's Festival event at the port, and is distributing handmade maps to visitors. This year, instead of one exhibit on the port, individual houses will display their own dolls, as in days past when people went from house to house to admire the doll exhibits. But this time, Shinobu is asking people to turn the tiered exhibits toward the window, so visitors can walk through the neighborhoods and admire the displays from the road. This removes the pressure of having to entertain guests inside the house. Tea and candies are served outside on a table for those who wish to provide them. I have the nobleman's carriage and the ox cart I rescued from Eiko's box displayed in my window. The carriage set is just one part of the grand Doll Festival display that baby Emiko would have been given, probably by her grandparents.

Shinobu's husband, Takanori, is already reminding residents about the Boy's Day festival, suggesting they bring out their stored carp streamers to hang up around the port.

Kimihira will graduate from Shiraishi Junior High School in March and, in a strange twist of fate, the school has decided to stay open for one more year so that Kenshiro can finish his education on the island. Three full-time staff will stay on at the school and continue to commute from the mainland, and two part-time teachers will come throughout the week.

On April 21, the temple will hold a once-in-a-lifetime *shinzan-shiki* ceremony when the Buddhist Priest will officially hand over the temple to his son, the next generation. As the new Head Priest, Kanta's name will become, officially and forever, Kantai.

In May, an announcement will come over the island's PA system announcing Buddha's birthday and reminding islanders to attend the "bathing Buddha" ritual at the temple, when sweet rainwater is poured over the infant Buddha statue standing in a fountain.

When I stopped by to see Amagiso the other day, she was excited to show me the newly refurbished building next to her inn. "I'm starting a share-house!" says the eighty-five-year-old, hoping to attract temporary residents who want to stay on the island for two months or longer. The facility has two floors with four rooms facing the sea. There are beds, Western-style toilets, bidets and heated toilet seats. A large modern kitchen allows ten people to gather around the table. Outside, the BBQ area is right next to the sea.

I heard recently that Hime, the bewhiskered gentleman's beagle, passed away. On one of my evening walks, I saw the owner and expressed my condolences. "She was eight years old," he said. "Cancer." He invites me over for coffee, says he has something to show me. I am flabbergasted when I enter his house: Hime everywhere. Photos of the pup grace all her favorite places—Hime on the sofa, Hime on the bed, Hime next to her dog-food bowl. I'm ushered into a room where the gentleman's Buddhist altar is, where he puts out rice and tea for his deceased parents every day, lights incense and whispers a little prayer. And right there with them is a photo of Hime, smiling.

From my living room window, I still see him go out fishing in the mornings, but he no longer stops his boat in the middle of the port to bow to the eight-hundred-year-old rock-etched image of the deity Fudomyo-o.

Soon, the cherry trees will blossom and we'll sip sake under their boughs. Someone will bring a guitar and we'll all sing, and maybe even dance under the trees while perfect pink petals rain down upon us like snowflakes against the backdrop of the cerulean Seto Inland Sea.

❀ ❀ ❀

One morning, while rain tumbled from the sky, I glanced out my living room windows up to Tomiyama Hill. Haze hung among the studded pillars like ghosts rising from their graves. I spied a hunched figure under a black umbrella, a man, bent slightly in prayer, poised in front of Eiko's headstone. I knew immediately who it was.

A half hour later, he came through the door, water dripping off his jacket into pools on the tiled entryway of his old home. Lifting his eyes and with a grin so large it seemed to encompass a decade, he said, "I've come to pay my respects." So many years had passed, and now Eiko's son, a retired gentleman of sixty-five, had divested himself of his rain gear and was sitting comfortably on a cushion at the zelkova table in the living room. I put on the kettle for tea.

But I had been expecting him. It was the seventeenth year of Eiko's death, and I was sure he would come back for the seventeen-year memorial service. I didn't know exactly when he'd return but near the door I'd kept a box full of photos and memorabilia to entrust to him. He was thrilled.

We spent the afternoon going through the box while sipping tea. Among family-crested kimonos of silk threads, obi sashes of subdued hues, and under-kimonos delicately hand-painted with charcoal scenes of Mount Fuji, was a stack of photos that I had not looked through.

One in particular he wanted to show me. The small sepia photo laid ever so lightly in the palm of my hand. Eiko and two other

women from our neighborhood had made a pilgrimage to Kompi-rasan Shrine in Shikoku. The date on the photo is April 13, 1962. As the wooden shrine dedicated to mariners looms in the background, the three middle-aged women pose in front of its stone steps. Dressed in kimonos and erect on tall *geta* sandals, their obi sashes are covered by spring *haori* overcoats. Eiko occupies the middle position, the place reserved in photographs for the most distinguished person. Flanked on both sides are her companions, faces arranged pleasant-ly for the camera, their hair left to flop naturally to their shoulders. But Eiko's jaw is set, and her hair coiffed back in waves to expose her high cheekbones, dainty elongated nose and thin lips. One ear is exposed, as if she has just tucked her hair behind it before tilting her face slightly away from the camera, while looking penetratingly into the lens. Cradled in her arms is a doll, blonde and round-eyed, with authentic-looking hair tied back and perfectly curled bangs atop its forehead. Such Western-style dolls were rare in postwar Japan and considered very precious. Touched by this image, I couldn't help but think that the shrine and the little girl at Eiko's bosom with eyes staring out of its head so blankly represented all Eiko had lost to a war that destroyed so many lives and brought such hardship to the widows left behind.

We sipped green tea until the rain stopped and the mist had lifted. Then Eiko's son boarded the last ferry of the day leaving the shores of Shiraishi Island.